Awaken to the Self Above All Struggles

Consider what you usually think of as being the cause of pain or dissatisfaction in your life. Maybe a betraying friend, shaky finances, a difficult workplace, or perhaps a past issue that still punishes you? And why it is that with all you've done to shake this suffering out of your life, it still survives?

Now think about those moments in your life highlighted by happiness. Why are these seldom-enough times so temporary? Why should simply enjoying life seem so hard?

There *is* an answer to these questions that all of us have asked; a secret answer that at once dispels the darkness of a thousand defeats *and* that provides a Way to lasting contentment and self-renewing happiness. Watch how quickly your whole life changes for the better after you discover this secret answer! Here's a hint. Everything hinges upon your awareness of this one simple Truth:

> *Freedom from what is* unwanted *by you begins*
> *with awakening to what is* unseen *within you.*

The enemy behind your life problems is *not* who, or what, you *think*. It does not live outside of you, but dwells within your own present mind.

Without your knowledge, invisible psychological characters inhabit your inner being and make choices for you—choices that work against your *real* life interests. Applying this book's Higher Principles to your life helps you to expose and dismiss these self-compromising characters and reveals the Truth about who you *really* are. The freedom you've longed for follows. You'll learn to align yourself with Life's secret direction, which invites the greatest power in the Universe to take your side.

Welcome to the most extrao̶r̶d̶i̶n̶a̶r̶y̶ ̶a̶d̶v̶e̶n̶t̶u̶r̶e̶ ̶o̶f̶ ̶y̶o̶u̶r̶ life. You are about to meet an̶d̶ ̶d̶e̶f̶e̶a̶t̶ ̶t̶h̶i̶s̶ ̶e̶n̶e̶m̶y̶! Victory is guaranteed!

About the Authors

Guy Finley is the author of over eight books and books-on-tape, several of which have become international best-sellers. His writings are found in public libraries throughout the United States and his work is widely endorsed by doctors, celebrities, and leading professionals.

He has enjoyed numerous successful careers, including composing award-winning music for many popular recording artists, motion pictures, and television programs. From 1970 through 1979, he wrote and recorded his own albums for the prestigious Motown and RCA record labels. Guy is the son of late-night talk show pioneer and radio celebrity Larry Finley.

In 1979, after travels to India and parts of the Far East in search of Truth and Higher Wisdom, Guy voluntarily retired from his flourishing career in order to simplify his life and continue with his inner studies. He now lives in southern Oregon, where he gives ongoing talks on self development.

Ellen Dickstein earned her Ph.D. in Psychology from the Johns Hopkins University and has published many papers on issues such as the development of the self-concept and the internal sense of what is right. After being awarded tenure at Dallas' Southern Methodist University, she realized that the genuine answers she sought did not lie within traditional psychology and began her spiritual journey studying with noted self-development author Vernon Howard.

Currently, Ellen writes and directs an international self-study program for inner discovery.

WINNING THE WAR WITHIN YOURSELF

THE
INTIMATE
ENEMY

GUY FINLEY
AND DR. ELLEN DICKSTEIN

1997
Llewellyn Publications
St. Paul, Minnesota 55164-0383, U.S.A.

FIRST EDITION
Second Printing, 1997

Cover design by Tom Grewe
Editing by Laura Gudbaur
Book design and typesetting by Rebecca Zins

Library of Congress Cataloging-in-Publication Data

Finley, Guy, 1949–
    The intimate enemy: winning the war within yourself / Guy Finley and Ellen Dickstein.—1st ed.
        p. cm.
    ISBN 1-56718-279-8 (trade pbk.)
    1. Self-actualization (Psychology) 2. Self-efficacy 3. Self-defeating behavior. I. Dickstein, Ellen. II. Title.
BF637.S4F554   1997
158.1—dc21   97-15774
                                                          CIP

Llewellyn Publications
A Division of Llewellyn Worldwide, Ltd.
P.O. Box 64383, Dept. K279-8
St. Paul, MN 55164-0383, U.S.A.

I s it necessary we suffer over the things we do? Or . . . is there a transforming secret that I not only have the power to understand, but one with the power to lift me above *all* of life's storms? This question invites the Truth to end every pain, and within it we take our first true steps toward freedom.

Other Books by Guy Finley

Designing Your Own Destiny
Freedom from the Ties That Bind (also in Spanish)
The Secret of Letting Go
The Secret Way of Wonder
The Lost Secrets of Prayer

To Write to Guy Finley

To receive your free encouraging poster of helpful inner-life insights as well as information on Guy Finley's books, tapes, and ongoing classes, write to:

> The Life of Learning Foundation
> P.O. Box 10E
> Merlin, OR 97532

Help spread the Light! If you know of someone who is interested in these Higher Ideas, please send his or her name and address to The Life of Learning Foundation at the above address. The latest complete list of Guy Finley's books, booklets, and tapes will be sent to them.

Thank you!

CONTENTS

A Welcoming Note from Guy Finley

Have you ever noticed how some moments in your life stand out more than others? How some of these moments can seem, at least at the time, to be relatively unimportant in the overall scale of your life? And still . . . how it's possible to know *in that moment* you'll never forget what just happened?

Let me relate to you one such unforgettable moment of mine. It helps set the stage to explain some of the reasons for writing this new book, as well as what you can expect to find within its pages. The story begins years ago with me in the middle of a newspaper interview about my latest book at the time. At that point in our conversation, the journalist wanted to know what it was about my life that had brought me to write what she called "this kind" of book.

The intonation of her voice told me that she had neither love nor understanding of what was the very center of my life. Nevertheless, I tried to encourage her with my response, gently suggesting to her to consider that our lives may be something far greater than any of us can "think" about; and that self-investigation is a timeless pursuit with timeless rewards—beyond the capacity of even ten thousand books to reveal, let alone convey to their readers. Well . . . .

To paraphrase an old expression that goes straight to the heart of what happened next, trying to talk to some people about Truth is like trying to explain ice to a summer insect.

The journalist looked me up and down, drew a breath, and fired her next question at me—as if to let me know that *she knew* what I was *really* up to. This is the moment I won't forget. She spoke somewhat sarcastically, ignoring all I had tried to convey:

"Yes, I see. But tell me, how many *more* books are *you* going to write?" She continued, "I mean, don't you think that there's something wrong with just putting out one book after another . . . all about the same subject?"

Somewhat (but not altogether) surprised by this attack-in-question-form, I let her not-too-concealed accusation rest for a heartbeat or two in the growing space between us before I answered. Having been assailed in this way many times in the past—sometimes with news reporters, and more often taking call-in questions as a guest on live radio shows—what I always strive to respond to when being pounced upon is *the moment*—and *not* the negativity in the person who's asking the question. I try to use these charged moments to show—for the benefit of anyone "out there" who is awake and attentive enough to notice—that *no* question asked of you in one kind of spirit need ever be answered from a spirit of that same nature.

Refusing to answer any hostile question or comment at *its* level always reveals both the real content of that remark *and* that there is, in fact, a higher level of understanding above it. This discovery puts you in charge of *all* such sneak attacks, whether it's some person pouncing on you, or your own thoughts trying to tear you down! This truly self-empowering new kind of answer—in the form of a conscious non-action—and the inner work it takes to be able "to do" it is one of the important lessons awaiting you in *The Intimate Enemy*, and of course there's much more.

When the newspaper reporter brushed away my answer that memorable (for me) afternoon, in favor of her embracing her own already negative perception, she also kept me from explaining why I *do* keep writing books. So, let me share the reason with you, my readers.

To begin with, self-discovery—and the new self-knowledge it generates—has no limitations, no moment where there isn't the possibility for something Higher to pierce the soul and so reveal that everything that once was is no more because something greater now stands there.

This means that there is no end to what is Higher, to what is ever-above you; and that the ground of this immeasurable state of self awaits you *within* you. As this Discovery of discoveries dawns in you, in its light is revealed the greatest secret on earth: Life is its movement into you; and this movement of Life takes place within you. In other words, your real life is an *inner* journey.

As you begin to align yourself with Life's secret direction, your experiences in it, and of yourself, are transformed. Slowly, but surely, a whole—and new—kind of pleasure permeates what used to be even your most mundane moments. Boredom with life simply ceases to exist for you. You no longer worry about what you're supposed to be doing with your life because, at last, you begin to realize that Life already has plans just for you!

Believe me, there is no greater strength than knowing that everything Life brings to you is *for you* as well. As this wondrous Fact grows clear to you, old enemies either vanish or they're transformed into your allies. Precious energies once wasted in futile self-defense are turned into new powers for further self-exploration, but this is really just the beginning.

By learning to cooperate with what Life wants for you—which is to help you realize the New You that you've been seeking all along—your victory over the intimate enemy is assured. The New You that emerges from the ground of this struggle within yourself is as different as the mighty open-limb oak is from its tightly shelled acorn seed. I know this to be true, and so will you.

The insights and life-healing principles revealed in this book are rooted deep in Reality. Of this there is no doubt, but they are only as powerful as is your wish to explore them. Hands-on self-investigation is the key that turns all such written Truths into the transformational forces they describe, which brings us to the following necessary bit of brief personal history:

As a direct result of the new internal work these higher ideas make possible, my own inner life has gone through a number of significant changes. The ability to see what is for our continuing growth—and the nature of that which stands in our way of this inner development—as well as what's necessary to break through this limited level of self—is now *greatly* clearer to me. From this new-again inner clarity arises the new wish—and a revitalized will—to rewrite the whole inner story anew. For, in Truth, it is new again.

The chief problem with all of this new energy—and the waves of insight that ride it as eagles do the wind—is finding the time and best ways to most effectively explore and explain all the discoveries being produced in the wake of these internal changes. My task became to determine a way to deal with this burgeoning material, to see that it got out and into the hands of those individuals who are interested in real inner work, which brings us to an important introduction.

To help me accomplish what I felt was now being indicated by these new conditions, I asked a long-time friend and associate, Dr. Ellen Dickstein, herself a dedicated student of higher-self knowledge and a published psychologist, if she would consider helping me journal my new work. I'm grateful she agreed.

Dr. Dickstein immersed herself for months in many of my most recently recorded talks, took pages upon pages of notes and, after patiently spending many hours with me assimilating all of these selected materials, she began to assemble a working manuscript. Then, carefully selecting certain anecdotes from her own inner work to embellish the body of this work in progress, it was handed back to me for final revisions. *The Intimate Enemy* is the result of this effort. More than just an elaboration of my past themes, this work stands between what I know to be two worlds: the writings of mine before this time of new understanding, and those that are to follow.

In the body of this book, particularly beginning with one of the earlier chapters on the "temporary person in charge," you'll learn new definitions and read some unusual descriptions about many of the various invisible psychological characters that inhabit your inner being and have been making choices for you! These new terms are a necessity, just as it's necessary to redefine any

organism as more is discovered about its nature and origin. Let me add that this new psychological terminology
will seem completely natural to your sensibilities,
because there are parts of you that already detect the
presence of their invisible existence within you. *The
Intimate Enemy* brings these entities out into the light of
your growing awareness, where all the powers they now
hold over you become your new power over them!

If you're already familiar with my books, you will see
for yourself the reasons for this evolution. If this book is
your first reading of my work, then what is new within it
will be just that for you: a series of new and exciting discoveries within and about your self that not only opens
your eyes to what has defeated you in the past, but that
gives you the strength and confidence you need to walk
into a fearless future.

Finally, let me add this one thought. It holds both a
promise and a prediction:

Work with the principles in this book; boldly apply
them to your life; embrace them openly, and you'll invite
the greatest power in the universe to take your side.
When this happens for you, you will know two things—
both of which make you unconquerable.

First, in the words of Meister Eckhart, the great Chris-
tian mystic: "We are the cause of our own obstacles."

Secondly, as Mary E. Bain writes: "For all but who
strive, who will but use untried forces, unknown energies, there are un-gathered riches, un-heard harmonies,
un-won crowns, yea, an un-revealed heaven."

Foreword

What a great day it is when we sign a peace treaty with life! Think of the energy we waste every day struggling against people and events. We are meant to use that energy to enjoy creative and dynamic lives. Instead, like a country at war, we squander most of it on the continuous mobilization of alternating attacking and defensive forces.

Why do we feel compelled to do it? It's because we see life as a battlefield on which we are constantly besieged by enemies. A worrisome news story may threaten us on the economic front. A rude store clerk may assault our pride. A new gray hair reflected back to us in the mirror brings us up against the onslaught of time itself. Our concerns about the future and regrets over the past are constant invitations to new battles.

So, how do we sign a personal peace treaty? By realizing that life is not really our enemy, and never has been. This happens when we discover the true basis of all our problems. For as long as we remain misguided about the actual cause of our fight with life, the battles must continue. But for the individual who has the courage to see people and events in a new—true—light, everything can be different. That's what this book is all about. Its purpose is to introduce you to a revolutionary view of yourself and everyone you know.

The Intimate Enemy is based on the work of inner-life author Guy Finley. I have had the opportunity to witness the development of these groundbreaking ideas by attending his ongoing talks in Oregon and through personal conversations with him. Guy's approach is a completely new way to understand timeless truths. For the scholar of ancient and contemporary wisdom, it elucidates and expands on the great philosophical and spiritual systems. For those who sense the urgent need to explore psychological and spiritual mysteries in order to achieve a renewed and enriched life, it unlocks the secret door.

You are about to embark on an extraordinary inner adventure. Soon you will have an unshakable understanding of not only your own, but of every human struggle, as well as the proof of a Higher world, free of all such strife. You will meet astounding parts of yourself that you never knew existed. You will see played out before you inner dramas that until now have controlled your life without your knowledge. You will meet the real—and only—enemy: the Intimate Enemy. Best of all, with that Higher awareness the revealing ideas in this book will help you awaken, you will discover for yourself—within yourself—a New Self . . . one that has *already* won the war within you.

DR. ELLEN DICKSTEIN

1

> *If he falls in this conflict, then he falls*
> *by his own hand; for physically and*
> *externally understood, I can fall by*
> *the hand of another, but spiritually*
> *there is only one who can destroy me,*
> *and that is myself.*

— Søren Kierkegaard

AWAKENING TO THE SELF ABOVE ALL STRUGGLES

As long as we have been on this planet, wise teachers have shared great truths about the real cause of the pain in our lives. And all of them pointed in exactly the opposite direction from where we've always tended to look. The enemy is not what we think it is. The real adversary in our lives, that proverbial thorn in our side that leaves us aching and angry, and then sends us looking for someone to blame, is not what we have always believed. It is not something "out there." It's something "in here": an intimate enemy.

We can each name a hundred things that we think is the enemy, but the enemy is *not:*

- a friend who betrays you
- a shaky economic system
- a threatening boss

1

- some stubborn habit
- that rude driver
- a computer that won't work

These things are all conditions that we must deal with. But the real enemy is much closer to home.

Everyone senses what that intimate enemy is as soon as he or she hears the expression. We all know that self-tormenting voice of defeat that rings within our own minds. No one is as critical of us as we are of ourselves. We all know how we are besieged by conflicting voices that send us first one way and then another, and finally make us doubt every decision. No one sabotages our plans and happiness as we, ourselves, do. No wonder none of our victories are permanent. Oh, we may have "fixed" that enemy for a time. Perhaps a heart-to-heart talk eased our anxiety about that relationship, or an especially good job done at the office made that employer finally take notice; however, "fixing" that person *outside* does nothing to fix the problem *inside*. The unhappy nature that created the first enemy will just create another. It has to, because the inner dissatisfaction that projected itself outward to identify that first enemy continues to rule from within.

A little story helps explain this. One day a man was walking around his property when a stone slipped unnoticed inside the sole of his shoe. The stone was just big enough to set the man slightly off balance, and as he walked across an uneven area of ground, he slipped. Annoyed, but confident of his actions, the man immediately "fixed" the problem by smoothing out the ground with a rake and shovel, but the stone lodged in his sole continued to cause him a great deal of pain. Proceeding with his walk, and squinting his eyes against the growing discomfort, he failed to see the low-hanging branch of a tree ahead of him. Sure enough, he walked right into it and bumped his nose! Greatly irritated, he "fixed" this new problem by cutting down the tree. More annoyed than ever, and unable to think clearly because of the now persistent pain, he got angry with his hired man for letting all these dangerous conditions exist in the first place. The obvious "fix" for this problem was to fire him!

It is clear to us as observers of this man's story that the way he perceived his situation ensured that there would never be an end to his problems and "fixes." Why? Because the problems he "fixed" were only secondary outcomes. He never addressed the real cause at all.

Similarly in our own lives, we've been working very hard to correct conditions that are really no more than secondary outcomes, and not the real problem at all. We fight a daily war to protect ourselves against enemies that, in fact, never are responsible for the pain we feel. The resolution of all our difficulties lies in correctly identifying and then eliminating the "stone in our sole." To do this, we must embark on a journey of self-discovery that examines many hidden reaches of our being, leaving no stone unturned! When the journey has been completed, we will never see ourselves or the world we live in the same way again, and our new understanding will give us an inner strength that can never be defeated.

Discover the Hidden Forces behind the War within You

The unhappiness we feel is the bitter fruit of a lack of self-understanding. In our confusion we do many things that are self-harming. We do not deliberately hurt ourselves in this way; the true cause lies in hidden, unconscious forces. Throughout this book we will refer to these forces in a number of ways, just as they have been referred to in spiritual studies and classical literature for thousands of years. They've been called negativities, the powers of darkness, opposing forces, even evil spirits, just to name a few. The important issue is not what we call these forces of conflict, but that we recognize the fact of their existence. For regardless of what names we give them, they all refer to one thing: unconscious, mechanical forces that cause human beings to behave like thoughtless machines, driven to action without reflection or compassion. When and wherever we see men and women taken over by something stronger than their ability to resist, whether it be anger, fear, lust, or greed, these hidden forces are at work.

At the same time there are Higher forces that can also be in charge of the individual. Down through the ages these powers have been referred to as the forces of Light, Goodness, or simply the Truth: uplifting words that describe higher thoughts and conscious awareness that empower individuals to act and feel in a way that is genuinely good and true for all involved. These higher and lower life forces are in a perpetual battle for control of individuals. Portrayals of this battle between good and evil dominate the art and literature of all recorded cultures. But what does it mean for each of us personally? It means that at any moment we have a choice. We can choose to work to stay awake psychologically and spiritually and live from and within a superior self, or we can fall back into a state of psychic slumber whose chief feature is a life of fear, frustration, and fighting.

What do we mean by psychic slumber, and how does it affect our daily experience? In his book *The Secret of Letting Go,* Guy supplies a valuable glimpse:

> Intelligence does not cause itself to suffer. Yet, as proven, we suffer. This can only mean that a counterfeit intelligence has been passed off on us and its thinking accepted as our very own. There is only one way that such a sinister switch could take place within us and go undetected. During those all-too-familiar worry-packed moments, we are asleep to ourselves. In this strange psychic slumber we only dream we are awake, so can you see the solution to this sorry state? Since unawareness of ourselves is the only problem, then awareness is the only answer. A sting operation can only work as long as the victim believes that one of the players who is secretly in on the sting is trying to help him.
>
> You may not be able to think your way out, but you can see your way clear. This special kind of inner seeing is safety. Waking up to yourself is the same as letting go of all those self-defeating thoughts and feelings that have been telling you how to win.

Many people have unknowingly chosen to stay in psychic slumber for so long that they are no longer aware they even have a choice. Discovering that this choice is ours to make is one of the most exciting revelations greeting the new spiritual student. Unfortunately, as sincere as that student might be, choosing the Light is not a one-time decision that solves the matter forever. Until our spiritual strength grows, we are continually pulled back to our old self-defeating self. We must work diligently to catch ourselves in a state of sleep and try to grab and extend moments of consciousness when we can.

Thinking about ourselves in this way, as beings operated upon by forces of either light or darkness, of consciousness or unconsciousness, can help us to understand the battle that wages within us, and that is then projected outward. Dark, negative forces create fear, self-concern, and all the fighting that results. At the same time, the forces of Light are trying to show us that there is a higher world where we are always safe and where there are no enemies to battle. It is only wrong thinking that creates our enemies, and that sustains the view that our universe is a hostile place, a battleground designed to thwart our goals and dreams. Higher consciousness shows us that none of this misperception is real. And when we fully understand this, we also understand that there never really was any battle at all, not even between the forces of light and dark. The light is *always* victorious. The superior strength of Reality *is* that no lie can dwell within it. When our understanding of this is complete, which it will be when we reach the happy conclusion of this book, we will be well on our way to knowing the Truth about ourselves. Then all will be well, for we will also be free. And *this* is victory! As Sun-Tzu writes:

> One who knows the enemy and knows himself will not be endangered in a hundred engagements. One who does not know the enemy but knows himself will sometimes be victorious, sometimes meet with defeat. One who knows neither the enemy nor himself will invariably be defeated in every engagement.

Sure Guarantees for Swift Progress

The only higher facts that can transform our lives are those that have been made our own through firsthand experience. Until a child learns to walk for himself, he cannot move from place to place on his own, regardless of how many people he has seen walk. In the same way, memorized ideas woven into a person's thinking without any true understanding will be of no help during a crisis. Surface ideas that have not taken hold in a person's heart cannot grow and mature so that they touch all of a person's life with guidance and wisdom. Parroted ideas do not provide real strength any more than the word "sugar" painted on a lemon makes it sweet.

When you see a truth from yourself, however, through your own experience, it becomes a part of you. It proves itself to you again and again through more wide-ranging examples that you yourself discover, and it attracts other truths to it. With time your clarity of vision grows, and because it is based on Truth, it cannot be shaken. What starts as one right idea—a single drop of refreshing

water—grows to a generously flowing fountain that nour-
ishes and sustains you for life.

For this reason, great Truths have always been presented in the form of examples or parables that provide a
way for the listener to prove them through personal
investigation. As Guy puts it, the great masters have not
presented "teachings," but "showings."

In the New Testament, for example, Christ invited his
audience to look at some simple thing, such as the lilies
in the field or a mustard seed, and to take from it a pro-
found lesson about the nature of higher development.
When people grasped the lesson, they began a process of
reeducating themselves. They could use the "showing" to
reorient their thinking and transform the lesson into an
inner fact. For example, it might give them a deeper
understanding of the futility of worry, which they could
prove to themselves by applying the lesson.

When we use "showings" to discover more truths, we
learn how to teach ourselves. We learn how to learn.
Once we do that, the pace of our learning advances very
rapidly. Throughout this book, you will be presented with
new ideas in a way that enables you to prove them for
yourself. As you proceed, you will learn how to learn.
You will start to make connections between the things
you see every day and truthful principles. Then your
progress will be swift and sure.

New Facts for Real Strength

Let's start by trying to understand strength. Most people want very much to be strong, but do not seem to be able to find the real strength they yearn for. Instead, they find qualities that pass themselves off as strength, but secretly leave these people feeling weak. Here are some examples of false strength:

- lashing out in anger when frustrated
- demanding that we are right
- blaming someone else for causing the problem
- being loud and intimidating, or cold and critical
- feeling confident because of any contrived appearance

By contrast, here are some examples of real strength:

- remaining calm in a crisis
- never feeling the need to prove ourselves to anyone
- seeking to solve the problem rather than placing blame
- enjoying self-command regardless of uncertain circumstances
- seeing all setbacks as necessary steps to Higher success

Study these two lists and try to see their great difference, not only in the individual areas of strength, but also with regard to the whole human character from which they arise. What a different kind of life would be led by someone who displayed the qualities in the second list as compared to the first. It is possible for any of us to achieve that different kind of life, but only in proportion to our willingness to see the difference between real and false strength. Our growing understanding of the difference is key, for it brings about an inner change that puts us in an entirely new relationship with life.

We can all see that pretending to be strong just doesn't work. From our own experience with pretense we've learned that, eventually, life calls our bluff and we're revealed to be unequal to the challenge. And who hasn't suffered from believing in the pretend strength of others? We've all had experiences where we thought we'd found something or someone who would be strong for us, and then were betrayed. We thought we had something that would help us to be victorious over any threat, but at the crucial moment, it did nothing to prevent us from getting nervous or angry. We wanted to think we finally had something that would make our fortress invulnerable, but time and again those invaders of fear or worry breached the walls, causing us to suffer yet another defeat.

Now you are about to read some entirely new facts about real strength that may seem very different to you. Welcome these new discoveries, and then watch how your new understanding of strength and victory lifts you into a realm of peaceful power where self rule is sovereign.

The True View that Starts the Healing in You

Have you ever noticed how things grow? For example, how does a pearl grow? It starts with a tiny irritant, maybe a grain of sand, that finds its way into an oyster. The oyster slowly lays down layer upon layer of protective material over the grain of sand, and in this way the pearl is formed—from the inside out. What about a tree; how does it grow? You can see for yourself if you've ever looked at a tree stump. You can see the rings that show you how it grew from the inside out. A wound heals from the inside out. From cellular life to the expanding universe, everything moves from the inside out.

Guy points out that in all the world there seems to be only one exception to this immutable law of nature. And that exception is in how our usual misguided mind sees the world around it. When this sensory mind of ours perceives life, it mistakenly sees things as happening to it from the outside in. How does this error in perception affect us? It means that we perceive life as a series of things coming at us. Everything about us is oriented outwardly, and it appears to us that our lives are being determined from the outside in. We don't see the importance of our inner states—the ways in which the content of our thoughts and feelings actually determines how we interpret what we see. We believe that the things we see coming at us are either good or bad in and of themselves.

Then we believe we must make choices based on what we see coming at us, not realizing that our very interpretation of what we see is a choice we have already made without knowing it. So, in the mistaken belief that we're at the mercy of these external events, we then define strength in terms of our ability to meet and handle them. This is why our wars never end. They can't. When both sides of the battle are in one person, the only peace he or she knows is the temporary silence that falls between thinking that everything's handled and then finding out it's not.

What if we viewed things in a completely different way, and what if that different way were the correct way? Everything would change. Let's see how.

Correct This Mistake and Change Your Life

Life does not come at us from the outside in, even though that is the way we've always seen it. Once we understand this, we'll see the mistake we've been making all along about the true meaning of strength. Currently, we have a list of things we want to overcome: our past; our failure to acquire what we believe we need; a pressing world that has it in for us. We've identified these challenges as something that comes at us from outside. Naturally enough, our behavior is based on what our mind identifies as the cause of the problem. We keep fighting the exterior challenge as a means of healing ourselves, but we keep getting hurt. A wound that is covered over too soon fails to heal from the inside. In the same way, as we try to fix the psychological wound from the outside, we interfere with the natural healing process, which must be an internal one. Because we don't understand the nature of the wound, we rend it again.

For example, perhaps a woman believes that the pain she feels is caused by cruel men. She vows never to be hurt again. Her attitudes toward men become hardened, but at the same time she secretly becomes more desperate to find a kind man who will cure her pain. To her dismay, she continues to attract cruel men through the unconscious signals she sends out. The hardened attitude that she takes as her strength is really her weakness, and it perpetuates the problem. As long as she continues to look at her problem from the outside in, there can be no genuine solution.

We can see that she is making a mistake by looking at herself from the outside in, but what about us? Let's see what happens when we look at ourselves in this new way—the True Way.

Like all living things, each of us is in the process of unfolding, living, being, from the inside out. The way our minds work, our expectations—our personalities—determine the way we experience, interpret, and react to the events we meet. The same event—let's say, an eclipse of the sun—can mean entirely different things to different people. That's because for each of them, life is unfolding from the inside out. Thus, a learned astronomer sees the eclipse as an exciting event that can be mined for golden nuggets of new scientific information. An artist sees the event as one of mystery and wonder and makes note of the unusual lighting effects that can be used in future paintings. An uneducated individual living on an isolated South Seas island might see the event as a frightening ordeal, perhaps portending the end of the world!

Many different interpretations of the same event also occur on a less cosmic scale. Rising interest rates mean one thing if you're a banker, and quite another if you are in the market for a new home. Putting on a few pounds means one thing to a woman who is confident about her self-worth, and quite another to a woman who fears that the passing of her youthful beauty means the loss of her real value.

Over time, and in a process that we'll come to understand more fully in later chapters, there come to be formed in our minds and hearts certain incorrect ideas and mistaken beliefs about ourselves and our needs—just like that woman in our example above who had a problem with cruel men. These conditioned mental and emotional pictures are not who we really are, but they seem so real to us that they become the platform from which we view and interpret the events we meet. When events occur that disagree with or fail to confirm those ideas, we see them as threats. Now our attention moves outward. Instead of understanding that the event only appears threatening because that's the way a self-picture interpreted it, we believe that it is an objective threat—*an enemy.* Now we find ourselves in a constant battle to control external circumstances in order to protect the images. Events that are truly neutral in nature are interpreted to be a real threat, and so we go to war. The whole thing was the result of an erroneous inner reaction, not the external event.

The fear we feel at the possible exposure of our shaky images is a form of pain. This pain is caused by an undetected inner activity, but we project this disturbance outward and blame the event. Meanwhile, the genuine you, waiting to unfold from within, lies forgotten. Instead of learning from events, we take them as our enemy. Through neglect, the voice of the True You grows fainter until it no longer guides your life, while you go off fighting meaningless battles. The quiet power of your true inner nature is silenced, while the outer life stumbles forward, unable to find the rest in resolution that it seeks.

Have you ever seen a rosebud that failed to bloom properly from within? The outer leaves whither as the inner growth stops. The flower fails to unfold. For many people who enjoy the false excitement of these never-ending life-battles, life is like that thwarted rosebud. It gradually withers from without because it fails to fulfill its true purpose: to unfold into its full flower from within.

However, things can be different for the person who grows tired of fighting wars that have no meaning and that never reach a conclusion. One day your greatest desire will be to watch your life unfold fully according to its own higher plan. You will grow weary with your own idea of strength with its accompanying false excitement. You will gladly sacrifice it so that you may experience a Higher wisdom that will be strong *for* you. What relief you will feel in coming into the real self-command of realizing you never had to be strong at all in the way you always thought you did.

What would this new view of strength mean for the woman in our previous example? Instead of focusing her energy on trying to protect herself from the falsely per-ceived enemy of men who will hurt her, she begins to see that her real enemy is the intimate, invisible one buried in her false beliefs that: (1) without someone to love her she will never know real love, (2) unless she finds a man who will be strong for her, she'll always be outmatched by an uncaring world, and (3) that her happiness is dependent on something outside of her own True Nature.

With her new knowledge of the real enemy, she would no longer hate or fear anyone. Her true understanding of herself would also give her a new and compassionate understanding of others, including those who had hurt her before. With her new perception paving the way, she would never again get involved with a cruel man in a des-perate search for acceptance. For the first time, it would be possible for her to have a nice relationship with a nice man. Her life would have been healed from the inside out, and now her outer life would reflect the genuine strength and contentment of her developing inner being.

How to Make Problems Fall Away

When we see this world as a hostile place where new attacks are constantly launched against a shaky self, it only seems natural for us to be self-protective, and that's exactly what we do. We put tremendous amounts of energy into developing and carrying out our plans for defense. Thus, we justify our actions to ward off the possible criticism of others. We fawn before people we see as more powerful than we are. We tell ourselves that we are superior to those we see as less powerful than ourselves. So, instead of living our lives fully and freely, we suffer from constantly comparing ourselves to others while unconsciously hoping we can make ourselves into someone against whom others will compare themselves!

In a way, it's as though we have built psychological bunkers from which we peer out at the world, wondering from where the next attack will come. Whenever we find ourselves hunkering down in those bunkers, building our defenses and planning our attacks, it would be an excellent time to remember this new view of our lives: that we are actually unfolding from the inside out, regardless of the perception we have that the problems lie in threatening enemies that charge us from outside. This means that instead of putting our attention on what others have done or said, or what the news of the day is, we turn our attention inward. When we see the "attack" coming, we turn our attention around to see that it is only our false view that *perceives* an attack; and when we see that the "threat" we're about to battle is really just a shadow—cast off from a false idea we hold about ourselves—*then* we meet the event from our True Self; our own awakened nature whose higher understanding realizes that the perceived "attack" upon us has no power *of itself*. It is only our reaction to it, our belief in the insulted or hurt self it gives rise to, that gives it any power over us. In the past, we accepted the cruel remark of a thoughtless person as being something real, with the power to hurt us. Our wrong thinking created the problem, and therefore could never solve it. It was not separate from the problem. Now, as our new and higher awareness refuses to give our life energy to perpetuating the wrong thinking, the problem must fall away of itself.

To achieve this state, we must first become tired of fighting all these battles and trying to be strong from our own present idea of strength. We can be that rare person who says, "I won't try to be strong anymore. I'll just watch. I'll start to participate in my life in a whole new way." This means working to see that our life is created from the inside out. When our tricked perception sees something as threatening, we are tricked into another battle. When our conscious awareness sees that there are only passing events and does not get involved, there are no battles. The only critical issue is what unfolds inside of us. We cannot change, control, or be stronger than anything our mind says is outside of us; but we can be inwardly awake, conscious of the fact that we don't need to be stronger than what we see, because we aren't really separate from what we see. We just need to start seeing more accurately. Then, we will understand that there is another kind of strength altogether—a Higher strength—of which we can partake. Resting in that strength means we don't have to try to win anything outside at all.

Win Permanent Victory over
the Enemy Within

We've been introduced to some new and very challenging ideas in this chapter, but perhaps the strangest of all is that we ourselves are our only enemy. This closer-than-close enemy is a product of our misperception, and it is made up of the many conflicting parts within us that battle against one another in a warring world that they create. It is this enemy within that makes the world we see so mad and wobbly and causes all the inner pain we feel. Then, when we project all this pain outward, we identify people and conditions to blame and fight against instead of looking to the true cause inside ourselves.

Through many years of studies such as these, my own experience proves that the inner and outer warring will just go on and on for most people. They will cling to their unconscious selves, which means their conflict with and in life will continue. But for those who will choose to choose Real Life, all can be different. They can begin living from an interior and higher safe haven instead of from their feuding minds. They will have the courage to ask, "Is it possible I am my own enemy? Could it truly be that my own thoughts and feelings are against my own best self-interest?"

The following chapters describe, step by step, how this internal enemy operates so you can see it in action for yourself within yourself. You will also come to understand the invisible processes by which it is created and the way in which it grows and steals our energy. Then, through the clear light of understanding, you will see how it is possible to win permanent victory over this intimate enemy.

Special Summary

> Living from our present life-level, we are almost always nervous about what's going on around us. Why? Because we still live with the mistaken notion that who we are is somehow affected or determined by what happens to us. . . . This is why we are going to leave behind us, once and for all, this threatened nature of ours. By placing ourselves in the care of Real Intelligence, we can learn to let go of whatever it may be that has frightened us up to now.

——— Guy Finley
The Secret of Letting Go

2

> *There are moods in which we court*
> *suffering, in the hope that here, at least,*
> *we shall find reality, sharp peaks and*
> *edges of truth. But it turns out to be*
> *scene-painting and counterfeit. The only*
> *thing grief has taught me is to know how*
> *shallow it is.*

— Ralph Waldo Emerson

LET TRUTH TAKE YOU
BEYOND YOUR TROUBLES

Most human beings live life on a psychological battlefield because they don't know that another way of life exists just beyond their present understanding. This new way can be found and walked by any sincere man or woman willing to leave behind a familiar but painful path through life in favor of the new and true one. Truth waits patiently for us, working to show us through our daily experiences that seeing through our own ideas of "who" we're "supposed" to be is the same as breaking down the walls of hostility those same ideas have created and by which we are held captive.

What is the Truth? This question is not nearly as difficult as we've been given to believe. Truth is what is real, which is more often than not quite different from what our minds *tell us* is real. Truth is life experienced directly, not through the distorting veil of thought. It is the force of life itself, that *is* right now, and that *sees that it is*. It is closer than your heartbeat, and it is that which does the beating. Our minds cannot encompass the Truth, but the Truth encompasses everything. When we see the inadequacy of our own minds to see things as they actually are, that is the invitation to Truth to see life for us.

As individuals who seek a life of Truth, we must be wide open in all our attitudes, prepared to discard everything we thought we knew in a moment-to-moment inquiry to find out what is or is not true right now. As we throw aside our mechanical beliefs and embrace the search for Truth, the source of Truth embraces us and guides us forward on our journey of self-discovery.

A Truth seeker is someone who wishes to understand the reality of every situation, even if this proves that his or her original perception or belief was wrong. We begin to think like this: "Something happened to me today. I was taken over by fear. I fought with people in my own mind. I was tormented by memories of the past and doubts about the future. This has always been the pattern of my life, and all I ever thought was possible. But now I see that my resentment wrecks me, and my anger towards anyone only sets *me* on fire. I don't want this anymore, and I wonder if anything else is possible. I sense that there might be more to this life. I look at the night sky and see its beauty and feel its power. Is it possible for *my* life to reflect the order and intelligence that seems to be the rule everywhere, except within the clouded minds of human beings? Is it necessary to suffer, or is there a transforming secret that I have the power to understand?"

When we begin to wonder like this, there is a chance for genuine change. Our love of Truth invites its life-healing power. Then any event that teaches us about ourselves becomes good. Right in the middle of the storm, it becomes possible to question its reality and ask if it is necessary to be buffeted about helplessly. That question invites the Truth to end every pain, and we begin to take our first steps toward freedom.

New Light that Reveals and Heals Old Pains

It takes little effort to see how much we suffer. Look at people's faces, or read the newspaper. Everywhere people's hearts ache. Yet, if you ask most of them about their own lives, they will lie about their confusion and unhappiness. "No, I don't have any pain in my heart," they will say. "Look at how full my life is, look at all the people around me, look at all my plans to get even more."

Unless we accept the reality of our lives, nothing will change. We all have the same suffering, anger, doubt, anxiety over the future, and regret over the past. The specific ghosts that haunt us are particular to our own experience, but we all feel the same shakiness. We work hard to hide this from ourselves and others. We put forward our own masks and believe in those of others. We point to people who seem to have their lives in order and say, "Look at old Charlie. He's doing great. He never loses his temper, and look at how successful he is." No one wants to see that Charlie goes home at night and drinks to forget himself, or buries himself in the television; that he cruelly torments himself and his family in ways so subtle that no one recognizes it for what it is.

One way we preserve our masks is to avoid taking responsibility for our pain by finding some outside cause to explain it. We blame our depression on someone's thoughtless remark, or the weather. We justify our anger by pointing to someone else's careless stupidity. We never question the necessity of the reaction in the first place, let alone wonder whether the feeling might have been there all the time, and just emerged when conditions gave it an excuse to surface.

Is psychological pain necessary, or can we reach a place within ourselves that is beyond the reach of *all* punishing reactions? Are we meant to suffer from a ceaseless inner war whose struggles profit none, or is there a higher meaning to life—one that makes everything make sense? The answer to these questions is yes. Absolutely yes! And if you are sincere about questions such as these, and want the Higher Life more than you want to "win" wars, there is something you can do to start receiving the genuine answers that lead to complete inner victory, and you can start by doing something completely new with your old pains.

How to End Every Pain

The next time you experience any kind of pain—an irritation, a flash of anger, a twinge of resentment—you can do something that will turn it into a new and different experience. Inner-life master and author Vernon Howard explains an amazing method in Guy's book, *The Secret of Letting Go*. He writes that when the pain comes, we are not to think about it as we always do. Instead, we are to do something different, and that is to say, "I don't understand the pain." Each time you catch a pain admit that you don't understand it. You thought you did. You believed it was caused by another person or some event that thwarted you. As a result of those beliefs, you did many things to get rid of the pain, but it always came back. So now, admit that your beliefs may be all wrong, and simply say, "I don't understand the pain."

Vernon Howard explains it this way:

> When we complain and cry and moan and groan and think, "How did I get into this mess," etc., nothing will change. With this exercise, you are putting yourself in an entirely different department and you will receive the products that that department has ready for you. . . .
>
> Do you want the product of not having to make worried decisions all day long? Just say, "I don't understand"—this crisis or that heartache that just came up. AND STOP. GO THROUGH YOUR WHOLE DAY *NOT* UNDERSTANDING IT. . . .
>
> The majority of men and women sell their souls all day long in exchange for false, fleeting feelings of self-control. When you have true self-command, you never have to look for it or ever explain its absence to yourself.
>
> If you are willing to say, "I don't understand anything at all about my life," your false understanding will fall away and in its place will be the insight from Heaven itself.

This amazing method works by changing our fundamental relationship with both the pain and the Truth that can set us free from it. It means that we see that we've fought one losing battle after another with the pain, none of which has done anything to resolve it. We know our failure was due to our complete misunderstanding about the pain. So, now we will do nothing about it. In essence, by turning our pain over to the Truth, we're asking the Truth to show us the facts about our pain, which is the same as inviting Reality to rid us of it. And it will.

What a relief. Now we don't have to pretend anymore that we're wise or strong. Now we've turned the pain over to the right department and it can be handled by something other than our old, pain-based solutions. What an amazing revelation this is! It puts us in the right relationship with Truth. When we tried to handle everything on our own, everything we did perpetuated the pain. All we succeeded in doing was fueling its life with our own. Now we don't want to do that anymore, but we know that our old mind doesn't know any other way to respond to the challenges we meet each day. So, we stop making the familiar response and just go silent. We turn it all over to Truth. It alone can show us that we never had to do anything about the pain because it never had anything to do with who we really are. The brilliant philosopher Henri Amiel confirms our finding: "My true being, the essence of my nature, myself, remains inviolate and inaccessible to the world's attacks."

So, for now, just remember this: admit that nothing you've ever done has brought you the peace you say you want. The pain always returns. Therefore, maybe you don't really understand its cause as you thought you did. To find out the Truth, just stop doing everything the way you have been, and instead simply say in full honesty, "I don't understand this pain." Then wait for the exciting revelations that Truth will show you. Don't listen to the false voices that try to accuse you of taking the easy way out. It's just the opposite. We take real responsibility for our pain when we stop trying to deal with it in the old way, and instead try to understand it in a new way.

Go from Storms to Sunny Skies

During one very special Sunday study group, Guy told a wonderful story that explains a great deal about receiving higher help. It went like this:

Many years ago a group of voyagers traveling in an old wooden ship were caught in a stormy sea. Tossed against hidden reefs, the ship finally ran aground, and the people found themselves washed up on a desert island. In great anguish over their fate, they fought with one another and blamed all the forces of the universe for their sad condition. With time, however, they settled in, building their little shelters and scratching a bare existence from the earth. Eventually, most of them even forgot that there had ever been another kind of life off the island.

There was one man, however (we'll call him Joe), who never forgot that the island was not their home. He knew it was imperative that they do everything possible to attract rescue. So every night, without fail, he went to the island's highest point and lit a signal fire. He did this for many years, and after a while his fellow islanders began to mock him. "No one will ever see that fire," they told him. "No rescue will ever come. It's not so bad here. Why don't you just settle in like the rest of us and forget about all that nonsense?" But there was something in Joe that could not forget. He knew he would never be happy on the island. Rescue was his only hope. So, every night Joe built the fire, even on stormy evenings when it was especially difficult. Everyone else would stay huddled in their little shacks, but Joe would force himself to go out and light the signal.

One night the biggest storm anyone had ever seen tore across the island. Joe looked out through his doorway in despair. Everything inside of him told him not to go out that night. It was ridiculous to even try to light a fire in this driving rain, let alone hope that someone might be out there to see it, but Joe felt he had to make the attempt. So, weary at heart though he was, he gathered his equipment and trudged up the hill to try yet again. As he stood there, warming his hands in the fire that had taken so much effort to build, and looking out to sea, what should appear before his unbelieving eyes but another light. A ship was out there!

Joe ran to get his friends, but no one wanted to get out of bed. The only one who would come with him was his faithful wife, who for all those years had sent Joe off with a little snack to see him through each lonely night. The two of them ran back to the beach, and sure enough, a row boat was waiting there with six men at the oars. "We

saw your light," shouted one of the men above the crashing waves. "Get in and we'll take you back to our ship."

"Wait," Joe called back. "Let me try to get some of the
others."

"There's no time," the sailors urged. "The storm is getting worse. Save yourselves and get in the boat *now.*"

Joe and his wife knew it was no good to try to get the
others anyway. After all these years they didn't want to be
rescued. Joe suspected that they even enjoyed the pain of
their struggling existence. So, without looking back, the
relieved couple jumped into the waiting boat and made it
safely back home.

What about you? Doesn't it feel at times as though, like
Joe and the other unfortunate passengers, we are all ship-
wrecked on an island of confusion and stormy emotions?
That we've all but forgotten it's possible to live any other
way? Where our days are spent cursing the storms and
building inadequate shelters to protect ourselves while
doing nothing real to get rescued? Something in us
knows that there will never be an end to battling storms
on an island that sits directly in the surge of their path.

Joe represents those higher parts of us that sense there
is something outside of the storm. It is that right part that
knows our only hope is to be rescued, and that it is our
responsibility to invite rescue by sending out the signal.
Fighting the storm by resisting its winds and rain will do
no good. Truth tells us, "Resist not evil." Instead of battling life's storms, place your attention and efforts where
they can work for your true best interests. Seek the rescue
of True Understanding.

We all know what Joe felt like on that last stormy
evening when everything inside of him told him the
attempt to build a signal fire was useless. If you've been
studying truthful principles for some time, you may be
familiar with that betraying inner voice that tells you if
there were an answer, you would have found it long ago.
Don't listen to that voice! It's the voice of your false
nature, desperate for the continuation of itself. There is
only one thing that is important, and that is to be rescued. No matter how long it takes, once that rescuing
understanding comes to you, the time it took to arrive
will be immaterial. The only important fact will be that
you will know you are going home.

Let's see what all this means with a practical example.
Perhaps a man is worried about the future. He believes
that in order to feel secure, he must acquire a certain
amount of money. Any time he feels thwarted in his
efforts to achieve his aim, he finds himself in a storm of
anger and despair. But he has been working with these
ideas, so he decides to do something different about his
pain. When the worrisome thoughts come, instead of
coming up with some new scheme to protect himself, or
ranting against an unfair world, he decides to admit that
he doesn't know what to do, and instead, to light a signal
fire. That is, he asks for Higher help. As that light shines
on the storm, he begins to realize that he had been
putting himself through unnecessary torment. He sees
that his fear made demands that practicality did not
require. He sees that his desperation made him do foolish
things with his money, but that more intelligent decisions

were possible. By having the courage to see that everything he believed about himself was mistaken, a new, higher view is possible for him.

Stop fighting the storm. Instead, seek to understand it. When you begin to doubt everything you believe about your suffering, you will see that you never had to remain in the path of those destructive storms at all.

Regain Your Right to Be Self-Ruling

Many centuries ago a country in the far east was besieged by many natural disasters, such as floods and earthquakes. As a result, sickness, famine, and much unhappiness reigned throughout the land. The king of this country was sorely troubled, for he did not like to see his subjects suffering. Gathering his wise men around him, he explained, "My people are heavy-hearted. They don't understand all these difficulties that have assailed them. I need to tell them something that will comfort them and help them to withstand these trials."

The wise men said to the king, "There is a great Truth that will have the effect you desire. Tell your people, 'This too shall pass.' "

These simple words proved to be a balm for the king's subjects, as it is for all spiritually minded individuals seeking to understand their true meaning. They offer a tremendous insight into the nature of life, and specifically into the things that trouble us. The person who understands *why* all things must pass, and why their passing need leave behind no painful wound, can truly live in a higher world. These deeper meanings will become clearer to you as we go on to investigate a "knotty problem."

Have you ever gotten angry at a knot? Of course you have. You couldn't get your shoe lace undone, or clear that fishing line. A knot in a thin gold or silver neck chain can be especially difficult. When you fight with a knot you feel frustration. Now, if you think about it logically, clearly the knot has no intelligence of its own with which to thwart your intentions or make you feel angry. Yet when you fight with it, you fall under its power. You feel yourself to be at the mercy of the knot.

Since the knot itself has no power to act upon you, where is the power coming from that puts you under the influence of the knot? From one place only: your perception. Your perception of the knot is the only power it has, and that power is not in *it*; it is in *you*! You cannot be free of the frustration or anger you feel in not being able to untangle the knot until you learn to separate the fact of the thing from the power of it. It is a fact that the rope has a knot, but it is not a fact that the knot has power. It is your perception that attributes power to it.

We frequently feel ourselves to be under the power of things. We feel we are the victims of an unfair social system, economic upheavals, painful relationships—even a lawn chair that won't unfold right. We fight these conditions, feeling ourselves to be under their "dark" influence. The fact is, however, these events do not exist as negative events except for our perception of them. The only power they have is the power *we* give them. What is the proof? Someone else observing the same event may not see it as negative at all. If we separate the facts from what we perceive as a thing's power, we are on the way to freeing ourselves from all things that bother us. Your wish to understand your pain by shining the light of Truth on it will show you where to break the thought connection through which you give your life energy to events that would otherwise have no power over you. If you truly wish to be free, you can even shine that light back into what feels like your own hard or cold past, and the warm light of Truth will melt all those long past difficulties dwelling there until eventually nothing about your life will have the power to bother you again.

You Can Conquer Any Condition

Any event we see is really a temporary conjunction of a number of different conditions. If any of those conditions is lacking or different, the event is no longer the same event. Let's look at a simple physical example of this. Think about a chocolate cake. That cake results from the combination of a number of ingredients. If you take out any one, the cake is not the same. If you take out the chocolate, it's a vanilla cake. Take out the flour and the texture is completely different. The same if you take out the eggs. The whole event that is called a "chocolate cake" requires all the ingredients, or it is something else.

Now, let's apply this same principle to a psychological event. Perhaps it's anxiety over a relationship. The negative event that the anxious individual sees is made up of a number of different elements. Remove any of them, and the event changes. What might some of these conditions be? Could you have that negative event without that person having done what he did? No. Could you have it if the first person didn't have some kind of expectation about what the second person should do? No. Could you have it if the first person didn't believe that his or her happiness was dependent on the other person? No. These are just some of the conditions that create the negative event. The event is really nothing more than a temporary conjunction of those conditions. Something has been created that seems real and solid to the anxious person, but the perception of that anxious person is one of the elements in that temporary conjunction of conditions that makes it painful.

For that anxious individual, let's say it's a woman, her perception of a series of events has produced something to which she now gives power, but which she sees as having power over her. Her perception ties her to the event, and because of that tie, the event becomes self-perpetuating. In her eyes, the situation grows in strength and power to hurt her. She cannot see that if she withdrew her attention from it, it would lose every bit of power that it had. This brings us to an important finding, one we mustn't deny if we wish to win the war within: in one way or another, and to various degrees, we have a peculiar love affair with our own suffering.

The Secret Understanding that Makes Painful Events Disappear

We may deny that we value our aches, but on the other hand, we think about them all the time. We have yet to recognize the fact that our thinking about any painful event as something real, solid, and unavoidable is one of the conditions that perpetuate it. Take one thing out of the conjunction and it is no longer the same event. When we stop giving our life energy to any moment that seems overpowering, it loses its illusion of power. In that moment is also lost our prior belief that we have to submit to its punishment.

This shows us that no negative state or event has any individual, independent existence. We can begin to free ourselves from the event when we understand the truth about its power over us. Until now, we thought *from* our suffering instead of *toward* our suffering. Now, however, because of our new understanding, we can see through our suffering instead of through its eyes. And what a world of difference this difference makes! As author Maurice Nicoll confirms:

> Nor do we think that many of our insoluble difficulties, perplexities, and unanswered questions exist *because of the kind of consciousness* we naturally possess, and that a new degree of consciousness would either cause our awareness of them to either disappear or bring about an entirely new relationship to them.

What we see is that our perception produces what we experience, and our experience is made up of many different small elements that by themselves mean nothing. When our perception combines and organizes these events, and connects itself to them through an expectation or desire, the thing takes on a kind of life. It appears to us as a whole, dark, permanent entity that has the power to hurt us, but it isn't that at all. It's only a conjunction of events that has conditional dependence, and the primary condition that gives it power is our perception. When all these conditions are stirred up and "baked in a cake," that cake has reality to us. But in fact, the cake is made up of individual facts that will simply pass if we let them.

Why have we not seen this for ourselves? Why have we not let those facts just pass by without grabbing onto them? It's because we have become so used to being in a storm, we aren't at all sure who we are without something to suffer over. As strange as it may seem, we welcome the painful experience because *it makes us feel real.* But who is it who feels real? It's the false self—the intimate enemy.

Can you see what good news this is for those of us who wish to free ourselves from false suffering and find the Higher Life? It means that all those conditions that seemed so real and painful are just the creation of faulty perception. Our belief that the event had the power to hurt us is what made it so punishing and continued its existence, but now we understand that if the events are left to themselves, they must move on. The expression "This too shall pass" is now revealed in all its Wisdom.

Every temporary conjunction of events must pass as long as we don't keep it going through our own thoughts.

The bitter cake can't exist if one of the ingredients is displaced. In our own lives, we have kept the achy cake baking; but now that we see the facts, we no longer need to be a victim of our own misunderstanding. We can inwardly say to that suffering state, "You are not a power. You only feel like one. The knots in my life that have me all tied up have no power over me outside of my own misperception, but now I will learn to see things as they really are."

Now that we know negative events are not powerful in themselves, we can turn away from what we perceive as permanent punishment toward what can be called permanent pleasure. This is the same thing as turning toward Truth.

Everything passes. There is great beauty in this, both in the passing of pain *and* in the passing of pleasure. When things present themselves to you as permanent, don't believe it. Exercise a reasonable doubt. Discover from your own experience that the negative event that seems so overwhelming is not the power it presents itself to be. As your perception changes, a critical ingredient in the cake will change, and then the entire cake must change.

Put the Universe on Your Side

Every day we are attacked by a multitude of pains, so frequent and so familiar we don't even question them. In fact, we accept them as friends, as something to occupy us. These pains can range from petty irritations, to the anxiety we feel every time we write a check and see our bank balance decrease, to concerns about our health. One of the major sources of pain involves other people and our relationships with them.

Every day the storm comes. Some days we handle it better than others. Some days we can't handle it at all, and we have a breakdown. But no matter how many storms people face, and how many breakdowns they have, in most cases people put on a mask and claim that their lives are okay. They declare that they are in control, and even resent the fact that the question could have come up. One thing they do to convince themselves that all their emotional reactions make sense is to blame outside situations for the pain they feel. When things get too bad they may give up the "I'm in control mask" and put on the "I'm depressed mask." This too is only a mask and not an honest self-appraisal, because the person is still blaming the wrong thing for causing the state and failing to take real self-responsibility.

These conditions can all be changed, but only if we are willing to admit that these revelations about our inner natures are true. We must pierce through to the heart of the Truth ourselves so its strength becomes ours. We can start by admitting that the storm comes and knocks us down every day. Then we must find the courage to admit that we must change the way we meet life. At that point, we are willing to ask Truth to show us how, because we realize that we've always been wrong in the past. Rightness does exist, and we can be a part of it when we stop defending everything that has made us suffer.

Think of something that has been troublesome to you today. Perhaps you've tormented yourself over the question "Should I or shouldn't I?" Has it ever occurred to you that even that question might be an unnecessary pain? Isn't it the case that what we really want to be free of is the pain we experience when we try to decide what to do to be free of the pain? Or what about the pain we feel when we're concerned about what other people think about us? Have we ever questioned why it matters what they think, or whether what they think will really change our relationship with ourselves? We get upset when other people don't treat us as we think we deserve, and fail to see that the pain we feel has nothing to do with them, but is self-inflicted. These are the lessons that our pain can teach us. When we welcome the lesson, we can see that it was we ourselves who caused the storm that we say we have to battle.

The experience of every moment of our life is a direct reflection of our nature. We never experience anything that does not arise directly from our own inner life. Life always happens from the inside out. What we know and perceive and look for is what we get. The pain we feel as we enter a room and move self-consciously from the door to the chair is a reflection of what is in us, and not what is in those people we see before us. The fact that we have those pains is proof that we don't understand what our pains are about, for if we did understand, we would no longer tolerate their presence in our psychic system.

Life really is a special kind of journey that each and every day can present new vistas to our eager perception. Instead, we live in an unhappy world created by our *misperception.* Yet one of the marvels of our lives is that they can undergo a natural healing process when our wish for an awakened consciousness allows the Truth to shed its curative light. When that happens, even our pains become marvelous, because each one provides a fresh opportunity to learn more about what we have been doing against ourselves. This new knowledge gives us the power we need to cease this self-betrayal forever.

The realization that there are parts of us that are against us can hit us with a jolt. But when we see that these wrong parts have actually created the pains that they then falsely promise to free us of, we eagerly seek— and find—the real Friend who will bring all pains to an end. Only the Truth is on your side. When you live from the Truth, the whole universe will be on your side as well.

Special Summary

> *The pain of knowing that we don't know what to do is only entered once, while the pain of pretending that we do understand lives on for as long as the pretense.*

—Guy Finley
The Secret Way of Wonder

3

> *You cannot prevent the birds of sadness from flying over your head, but you can keep them from building nests in your hair.*

— Chinese Proverb

POSITIVE STEPS TO DROP NEGATIVE SPIRITS

Most of us have that unsettling sense that no matter how happy we may feel at any moment, a negative state is never too far away. It is always lurking somewhere in the background, just waiting to take us over. And when it does, it threatens our jobs, our relationships, and our spiritual efforts. Is it inevitable to live like this? Or are there positive steps we can take to drop negative spirits? The encouraging news is that there *are* definite steps to take, and all of them are based on our increased understanding of what negativity really is, and the unseen harm it does to us.

We've been taught that we have to tolerate negativity. We tiptoe around others when they're in the throes of a negative state, and we accept our own torments, hoping only to be able to cope. Parents desperately look for ways

41

to deal with the negativity in their children. We coddle these wrong, self-harming states for two reasons. The first involves self-love and self-protection: because we don't know better, we embrace the negativity as our own and therefore feel it should be defended. The second reason is secret fear: we're afraid of negativity, which means we resist it, and as we saw in the previous chapter, that resistance gives it our life-force. The solution is to understand the essence of negativity and then to learn how it operates in the dark.

Our new understanding begins by volunteering to get a lot tougher on ourselves—*and* on what's been so hard on us. Meekly submitting to any negative emotion in the hopes it will run its course and leave us alone just invites it to subjugate us again . . . and again. We can learn to do much better than to just automatically become angry or depressed every time events run counter to our expectations, and we can begin by gathering a few freeing facts:

Fact 1: *Negativity is opposition.*
When we're negative, we're opposed to life as it presents itself. We've labeled a particular outcome as bad, but in reality, life is not divided up into good and bad any more than the ocean is for or against its own waves.

Fact 2: *Life is whole, and it's all good.*
The events of life are reflections of broader patterns that are beyond our ability to see. All of them are in the interest of growth and development, and all of them, perceived correctly, serve to help us realize just how much the universe really is on our side. When bad things seem

to happen, it is not that the event is bad of itself. It is that we do not see the wholeness, and instead judge the event from our own limited and divided point of view. The negativity produced by our own judgment hurts us and keeps us from experiencing the good.

Fact 3: *Every time we accept a negative state we compromise ourselves and increase the level of conflict for ourselves and everyone we meet.*

Strangely, we accept the negativity because it gives us a powerful sense of who we are. We feel falsely energized by our sense of a separate self, apart from the wholeness. We even value our negativity because it makes the boundaries of our selves seem so strong and real. "I may be unhappy," we think, "but at least I know who I am and I know what my life is all about." But what we "know" is a false self-image, and what we think our lives are about is only an endless battle to protect something that was never real in the first place.

The evidence is all around us! Almost everywhere you see unhappy faces reflecting anger, self-pity, defeat, and other dark states. How much effort do we go to in order to make ourselves look good to others? Do we ever think about what the expression on our face says about us? Or how any negative spirit within us can undo all the good effects of everything we do to make ourselves physically healthy? One of the tricks of the intimate enemy is to make us believe that something that is destroying us is good for us. See negativity for the monster it is, and you'll want to be free of it forever. And you will be!

Catch Hitchhiking Spirits
in the Act

During one class meeting, Guy promised that the next
time we met he would tell us a story that would unmask
negative states as the intruders they are. We all eagerly
awaited the next class, and were not disappointed, for
this is the story he told:

One afternoon a traveling salesman found himself in a
small town, and decided to stop over. Almost at once he
noticed something strange about the place. The streets
were deserted and everything seemed to be in disarray.
He soon found out why. All the townspeople were at a
carnival that had been set up at the outskirts of the vil-
lage. Having nothing else to do, the salesman decided to
walk over to see what this carnival had to offer.

As he wandered through the various side shows, he
noticed that just about everyone was standing in line
before a particular attraction. It appeared to be a booth,
and the sign in front proclaimed "Twenty-five cents. See
the monsters through the peephole!" Intrigued, he
watched as one by one, each person in line looked
through the peephole, shrieked, and ran off. Eavesdrop-
ping on their conversations, it became apparent to him
that everyone was seeing something different. Extremely
curious by now, he decided to see these monsters for
himself. Getting in line, he moved forward slowly with
the rest until finally his turn came. Looking through the
peephole, he saw a most peculiar beast. Although it gave
him a shock, at the same time he felt oddly fascinated

and drawn to the monster. As he walked away stunned, he noticed that the line kept reforming as people got back on. He did too.

While standing in line, the salesman asked a man next to him how long the carnival had been in town. As the man replied, he seemed surprised himself at the answer. "Why, I'm not sure, but I'd guess it's been about three years." The salesman was shaken as he realized how long these people had been captured by this thing. Here, Guy broke into the story and told us that we have to let the things we see shake *us* up, like seeing we've been repeating the same self-destructive behavior for three years, carrying grudges for thirty years, or suffering from certain anxieties our entire lives. We've been embracing something harmful to us all this time without knowing it.

The salesman knew that something very strange was happening in the little town, and he was not immune to its fascinating hold. He even caught himself making plans to extend his stay. His interest had been captured. What was going on here? How could there be so many different creatures? Why was their draw so powerful? He decided to investigate.

After the carnival closed that night, he worked his way back behind the popular attraction. Entering through the unlocked back door, he saw nothing behind the peephole other than a large free-standing mirror. What!? His mind raced as he realized that the monster he had seen through the peephole had to have been his own reflection! Even as he reached this unthinkable conclusion, the back door creaked open and in walked the old caretaker.

"Pretty amazing, isn't it?" the old-timer said.

The salesman was speechless, so the caretaker continued. "You're the first person in this town who's come back to see what this attraction is all about. What we have here," he said, pointing to the mirror behind the peephole, "is a kind of magical reflector that reveals things that are happening inside of people." He paused for a long breath, and then looked directly into the man's eyes. "This reflector shows the hitchhiking spirits that take over the hearts and minds of human beings. Of course," he continued almost casually, "these spirits have no life of their own. They steal their life from the unwary men and women they attach themselves to." The salesman's mind was reeling. He didn't want to hear anymore. It was all too disturbing. Shouting, "This is all nonsense!" he ran back to his hotel room.

When he got back to his room, he found that the air conditioning was broken, the desk clerk was nowhere to be found, and there was no place to get anything to eat. Getting more and more negative, the salesman paced around his room. As he did, he walked by the dresser mirror, and out of the corner of his eye he saw something hideous. Here, Guy broke into the story once again and commented that when we're upset we don't like to look in the mirror. We don't like to see ourselves when a hitchhiking spirit is upon us. Seeing himself in the mirror gave the salesman yet another shock. He realized that everything the old caretaker told him was true, and that he was capable of being taken over by dark inner states set against his own True interests. Now he knew what he must do.

The salesman returned to the carnival to find the old caretaker and learn more. The old man told him, "You must understand hitchhiking spirits. They have no life of their own. They're not real. *You* make them real. They cannot live without your permission." The salesman protested, "But I *don't* give them permission. I *hate* them."

The old man smiled to himself and went on. "Hatred of them is one of the secret ways by which we embrace these negative states. We hate them because we think they are us, instead of something that we can just let pass through. Saying 'I' to any dark condition only empowers it. So you must stop embracing negative thoughts and feelings." Then he smiled again and chuckled quietly, as though he'd told himself a good joke. "I guess you could say, 'Bye-bye to negative I.'"

So, the salesman stayed for a while to find out what else the old man had to teach him about freeing himself from these psychic intruders. He gratefully learned and applied the lessons the old caretaker taught, and with his new wisdom he won a new life for himself.

Don't let hitchhiking spirits come in and take over *your* life. Learn to see through their tricky and tormenting deception. As a special light to help brighten your way, remember that not wanting to feel bad is a way of embracing feeling bad. Resisting the unhappy state *is* what gives it your life force. Try this new and higher action: the next time you feel a negative state like anger or depression, don't fight it. Instead, withdraw your permission by coming awake and going silent. See it for what it is, and don't give it your life energy. Catch the hitchhiking spirits in the act, and don't stop to pick them up!

Get to the Bottom of What's Betraying You

We each have ideas about who we are, how the events in our lives should go, and how other people should treat us. We believe that if everything goes according to our plan, we will be safe. By the same token, anything that threatens the fulfillment of the plan is seen as an enemy. What might some of these enemies be? Other people who don't give us the respect we deserve; an uncertain future; embarrassing events that prove we are not what we claim to be. In order to protect ourselves from the potential attacks of these enemies, we direct our lives along a path that will allow us to be more powerful than what we fear. So we work to make money, excel, appear more intelligent—anything that will make us feel stronger than what we think has the power to punish us.

These actions never bring permanent peace, and this is why. That enemy we would overpower does not exist at all. The enemy is within; it is an intimate enemy; it is nothing but a creation of our own uninvestigated thought nature. A fearful self interprets a neutral event as being an enemy, and goes into action to protect itself. Regardless of the outcome of that action, the war continues; for as long as the fearful self continues to see enemies, there will always be new battles.

Let's look at an example. Perhaps you're reading a magazine when you come across an article on declining economic conditions. Suddenly, you hear a voice that starts as a whisper in your ear and sends a small shock wave all the way down to your toes. The fearful voice says, "What if things get worse and I lose my job?" Now this thought running through you has no real life of its own and would be harmless if allowed to simply pass through, just like the snatches of a song that pass through your mind and disappear. Instead, you make the mistake of embracing that thought and all the emotions that accompany it. You have been taken over by a hitchhiking spirit. It feels like the real you, and it feels as though you are under attack. Now, more thoughts and feelings are attracted to the gathering whirlpool and a new false self has been created. If a "defiant self" has been created, you make aggressive plans for self-protection. If a "weak, timid self" has been created, you slip into a state of fearful depression. In either case, your day is ruined! But *the entire event,* including the self that now suffers, was only a combination of thoughts, and nothing more.

When you hate or fear something, you are really only reacting to a thought, and this reaction creates a sense of yourself as being a hater or fearer caught in a real battle with a real enemy. You can never defeat any such feared enemy outside yourself because there is none. It is a creation of your own mind.

Pascal writes that "we are troubled only by the fears which we, and not nature, give ourselves." This can be very difficult to understand. After all, we think, there *is* a real enemy when that economic condition leads to a pink slip on the desk. Yes, there may be a pink slip on the desk that may require us to take certain practical action, but what we see is not just the slip. We see a whole series of thoughts connected with an image we have of ourselves.

"I'm a failure," we say. "People will think less of me," we worry. So we create the condition in which a pink slip has the power to tell us who we are, or that others' opinions of us will go a certain way, and that what they think defines our worth. What good does it do to spend our lives fighting a battle we cannot win because both sides of the war are raging within our own minds? Our perception of the event is the event for us. When we perceive things from the point of view of a victim, everything becomes an enemy—an enemy that we ourselves created. When we no longer believe in the victim self, we can start to perceive life from our True Self, and then events take on an entirely different meaning.

The Hidden Message in the Mechanical Pumpkin

Here is an anecdote that Guy once told a small group of us over lunch. You'll see how it illustrates these ideas. He said that sometime during the Halloween season he and a friend decided to go to a restaurant for a meal. As they entered the small diner, they were startled by a wall-mounted mechanical pumpkin that jumped out at them while making spooky noises. It didn't take long to discover that the pumpkin had an electric eye that caused it to automatically lunge from its hiding place whenever anyone came within a certain range. Once they knew its secret, what had been a scary moment for the two of them became a funny one. They laughed at themselves, and, of course, everyone else who got scared by the "frightening phantom" that was no more than a mechanical toy.

It's the same with our minds. A thought comes by and somehow sets off the mechanical responder within us. Until we understand that both the scary thought and the scared self it creates are just figments passing through our psychic system, we have no control over the initial scary situation or the false self it creates to rescue us. But once we understand all this, we have a choice. When we realize that the "threat" never had any real power to hurt us, we are no longer compelled to produce an unconscious, automatic response of fear or anger.

You Can Be Stronger than Any Dark Spirit

As our growing understanding sheds more light on the dark spirits that have dominated us until now, we see through their illusion of power. Our victory over them comes not from defeating them in battle, but from understanding that they were never real.

Until now, we believed in and feared our negative states because we thought they were more powerful than we are. Anytime we fear something, it is because we think it is more powerful than us. Out in the open, we're afraid of a lion because we understand its superior physical power. We are not afraid of a leaf because we recognize it is powerless to hurt us. We can't fear something without thinking it has the ability to overpower us. However, in some cases, it is only our lack of understanding about the thing that makes us attribute power to it, and therefore fear it.

There are many things that are actually powerless but that still frighten us because we attribute power to them. The prime example is the dark. Darkness has no power in itself to hurt us, yet people fear it. Why? People fear the dark when they add something to it in their own minds. It's the relationship between them and what they've added that frightens them. We imagine things that could be lurking in the dark and then fear our own thought creations. It's the same with other negative psychological states that try to take us over, such as anger, fear of the future, or concern about others' thoughts about us. We attribute power to these passing thoughts and emotions, and our behavior then reflects either submission to the negative state or a struggle against it.

For example, suppose the negative state is depression. We submit to the state by going off to a corner and sulking; we struggle against it by running around looking for some distraction. Yet, regardless of what we do, the state continues because neither of these actions resolves it; to the contrary, these actions actually give life to a state that, of itself, has no real power. Everything we do to free ourselves only fixes the state. In fact, these states can never be resolved, but they can be *understood*; and when they are, we have the power to walk right past them.

One of the most difficult lessons we must face in our effort to win the war within ourselves has to do with the truth about our relationship with our own negative states: they fascinate us. That's right! But why do we value them so? The answer will surprise you.

We value negative states because of the strong sense of self we get from them. This may be very difficult for us to see, but a strong light will show us the freeing facts. No one wants to believe that he or she values things like self-pity, anger, and depression. We would insist we don't, and as evidence we point to the fact that we fight against them, but the struggle gives us a false sense of life and importance. It focuses attention on us and makes us feel like the center of a great deal of activity. The more we struggle, the more valuable these states become, because the more interesting and exciting they make us feel. We never feel our selves so strongly as when we are furious, or hurt, or depressed. Of course, this self is a created self, a false self. But it *feels* real, and that's why we cling to it. The power in the state is that by giving it our life, it feeds back to us a false sense of life and power. And as a result, we miss out on the Real Life we could experience if we were not filling ourselves with the false.

Can you see what we've done? We've unmasked the secret power of all negative states. A false part of us derives a sense of reality when it is bombarded by negative feelings. Because it values the sense of self it gets, it focuses attention on the state and feeds it our life energy. It builds up a structure of thoughts around the state that justifies it and keeps it going. All of this is done at the expense of who we really are. Our understanding of this deception gives us the power to win victory over these states because it shows us that we can do something else with those states that will reveal them to be powerless. Let's see what that something else is. . . .

The Power to Dissolve
Any Negative State

The next time you feel yourself slipping into a negative state, your new awareness of its dynamics will give you the "power" to unfix yourself from it. For example, perhaps there's something you want to do, but you're afraid that if you do it, something bad will happen. Perhaps it's getting up and giving a talk before an audience. Until now, you always thought there was no other choice but to be afraid—that somehow your fear protected you from fearful situations. Now, with your new understanding, you begin to see a number of crucial things. First of all, you're beginning to question your fear and how it could possibly be protecting you, when the only pain you feel is the fear itself. Second, you can now see that the main reason you value the fear is because of the strong sense of self it secretly provides. You know that you've always said you've hated those feelings, but now you see that your vibrating false self is glad to have any life at all, even a painful one!

Now suppose you've been asked to make a presentation to a large group of fellow employees. It's still weeks before your talk, and you see that you're caught up in nervousness over it, which you perpetuate by thinking about it. You see that there is no value in any of this, so you try something new. You refuse to give in to the feeling by sitting in the corner and shaking over it. And you refuse to struggle against it by putting on a false bravado and insisting you're not nervous at all. Instead, you just walk past it.

"Proceed while being afraid" is Vernon Howard's succinct instruction when faced with any scary obstruction. This means just move forward without paying any attention to the state at all. You're aware that the nervousness is there, trying to take you over, but you don't do anything with it. You stop feeding it your life energy. As a result, your experience of giving the talk is not at all as traumatic as your imagination had tried to tell you it would be, and you know that with your newfound understanding, you need never be as nervous again.

This new understanding placed into practice works with any negative state, from loneliness to anger or anything else. Don't stop to argue with it or deny it. Just go past it. You can do this when you understand that the only thing keeping you involved with the state is *you*. It's really all very simple, but only if we're willing to leave ourselves behind. We have to leave behind the false self that sees the state through *its* eyes and attributes it with power. We have to see that negative states have no business being in *our* business, and they won't be if we don't get fixed on them.

We must learn what it means to become unfixed from negative states, and we will when we realize that the sense of self we derive from them is worthless. It's not based on anything real, and it has no permanence because with time *all* states pass. Then, we are left exhausted, and fall prey to the next hitchhiking spirit that comes along. When the negative state comes, don't struggle with it or give yourself over to it. Instead, just go on with your life as though it doesn't exist, for it doesn't, not in reality. At night, when we fear the darkness, we flip on the light and everything that frightened us is gone, because the light dispels the frightening images in our own minds. When we flip on the light inwardly, psychologically, we see that dark states have no power outside of our fixation with them. When we struggle with them, we give them our power. When we give in to them, we allow them to dominate us. The only true alternative is to go on with our lives as though the thing were not there, and if we do that, it won't be there.

We've all seen this in little ways. Perhaps you felt depressed one day, and instead of giving in to it you went for a little walk, and sure enough, you felt better afterward. Why did you feel better? It was because feeling bad was a trick, and you just walked past it. Now learn the spiritual lesson from that and see that you can do the same thing inwardly. Walk past all negative states, and they must disappear.

Discover the Remarkable Power of Attention

One of the most potent weapons in the war within ourselves is the power of attention, and it can be wielded for or against our true interests. We've seen a number of times in this and previous chapters where the wrong use of attention can aggravate any problem. That very same power, however, used correctly, can reveal to us the truth about any situation and lead us to inner freedom. Let's examine the remarkable power of attention to learn how it works and how we can use it for real change.

Through the wrong use of attention we give power to emotions and ideas that would have no power of themselves. When our attention focuses on things that are wrong for us, like hitchhiking spirits, we actually invite them to take us over—in fact, we give them the power to do so. How does this happen? Guy has summed it up in two words:

Attention Animates

When attention is directed, it has the ability to invest an idea with energy and life. Wherever you place your attention, you give life to that seed of thought. You can see this in operation all the time. Has it ever happened to you that you had a thought, and soon discovered that someone else, a friend or co-worker, had a similar idea? It almost seems as though your attending to the thought gave it a life of its own and passed it to another person. We've all had something like this happen: you're stopped at a red light, and you look out your car window at a man passing by. You follow him with your eyes, and the next thing you know he turns around and looks at you! The power of attention almost seems to have a magnetic pull.

This power can be used for good or bad. When we use it for practical work, or for honest self-observation, we use it to our own benefit. However, when this power operates unconsciously to strengthen self-harming ideas, it becomes a barrier to natural strength, happiness, and love. At every moment, we stand on the threshold to a completely different and better life. If we become conscious of the true cause of our unhappiness, we can direct our attention away from its unconscious focus. At that point, something higher can come in to help us use the power of attention for our true good.

But first we must see how wrongly directed attention works against us. Perhaps a thought comes to you about a problem that's been bothering you. The thought takes an inner state and defines it for you by naming its "cause." Once the thought comes, your mind gives it attention. In that moment, you've animated that thought and given it life—and the life you've given it is your own! Here's an example of how this might come about. A man is walking through his office when his boss walks by and gives him a blank look. The thought pops into the man's mind that his boss is criticizing him or doesn't like him. He focuses attention on the thought, which strengthens it. He's convinced the boss has it in for him. The thought grows in authority for him, tormenting him for the rest of the day and causing him to snap at his family when he gets home. A hitchhiking spirit has been created out of the conjunction of a passing glance and misdirected attention.

Here is the amazing thing. This whole drama has been played out *inside* of the man, but not only does he not see its true origin, he believes it has been cast upon him by someone else—his heartless boss! He tries to get rid of the painful feelings by arguing with his boss, either outwardly or in his mind. The more he feels punished by the situation the more he wants to fight with it, thinking that its existence is separate from him, but it's not independent of him. He gave it its existence by unconsciously permitting his attention to be drawn to it. The more he resists it, the more it grows. The more it grows, the more he resists. The situation gets worse, and the worse it gets, the more he's convinced that the whole thing has been caused by something outside of him. Nothing can change until he begins to understand that his attention animated the thought, which he then wrongly fed with his own life. Only by becoming aware of this can he begin to use properly his most powerful weapon: attention.

Find New Strength in Awakened Attention

Now that we understand that attention animates, the solution to our painful problems becomes obvious: We must use our awakened attention to catch unnecessary thoughts and withdraw our consent from them.

We've suffered because we've unconsciously consented to painful thoughts. We've animated these thoughts with our own energy, and they have then been able to direct our behavior, leading us to fight, overeat, spend money, drink, and a thousand other self-destructive behaviors. By withdrawing our consent from these thoughts, we no longer animate negative energies. We neither resist them nor try to change them, two approaches that only seem to strengthen the problem. But withdrawing our consent is a method that cannot lose.

At the moment we feel a pain, we must notice where our attention is. We can use the pain to look back into our lives to see what we've been consenting to. This action separates us from the situation so we can see where our attention is. We see that for the past half hour we've been engaged in an imaginary argument with someone who isn't even there! We see that we've been animating painful thoughts. We suffer because we think about things that make us suffer. We get angry because we think about things that make us angry. Now we come to an amazing discovery: if I accidentally gave that negative spirit life, I can also consciously withdraw that life.

Until now, we've unconsciously allowed our attention to be carried by any passing thought, but now we will be attentive to where our attention is. As an exercise, several times each day we can break into our own thoughts and become wide awake to ourselves. For example, you might set yourself the task of trying to become aware of yourself and where your thoughts are every time you pass through a doorway. That evening, as you walk from your kitchen to your living room, you remember yourself as you pass through the door and realize that you're worrying about something you have to do the next day. You realize that there is no reason for you to be thinking about that at the moment, and that your worry has put you in an irritable mood. Your awareness shows you that you are not required to think those thoughts, and the mood they created is not real. You can refocus your attention and go on to enjoy your evening.

We've learned a great deal about the intimate enemy in this chapter. We've seen that negative states, like hitch-hiking spirits, are constantly trying to take us over, and that our fascination with them gives them the hold over us they seek. Once this occurs, a false self is created that perpetuates the negativity in order to keep itself going. It blames outside causes for the way it feels, but in fact the entire drama occurs within the person, and the primary power that keeps it all going is misdirected attention that focuses on the negativity and continues to feed it.

This inner war comes to an end when our own awakened nature causes us to withdraw our consent from the whole painful process. Instead of struggling against an enemy in a battle that cannot be won, we refuse, *consciously,* to be engaged in any battle at all. We simply walk past the enemy, which then must disappear, for the only life it has is what it can trick us into giving it.

When we drop negative spirits, our precious resources are no longer mobilized to fight an unnecessary war. We are filled with Real Life and Light, and we face each new experience with enthusiasm and curiosity; for life *is* whole and good when we are no longer surrounded by enemies that we ourselves created.

Special Summary

Our own thoughts may instruct us, without our ever knowing it, to cling to doubts; or to jump headlong into pools of self-pity. And because we don't know there's any alternative, we do as we're instructed.

What we don't know yet, but what we're learning even now, is that we can wake up right in the middle of these mental ordeals. Working with self-observation, we can actually see, for ourselves, that these self-compromising thoughts are just that: thoughts. They have no real authority, which means their unconscious direction does not have to be our destiny.

— Guy Finley
Freedom from the Ties That Bind

4

> *The very discovery of these hidden*
> *things is in itself a purifying experience!*
> *The soul needs to discover what is inside.*
> *The self nature needs to see what it really*
> *is, and what it is like—right to the very*
> *bottom.*
>
> —— Jeanne Guyon

MEET AND DEFEAT
THE INTIMATE ENEMY

Note: *The information that follows is truly revolutionary. In many years of both psychological and spiritual study, I have encountered neither better explanations nor solutions for all of the confusion and unhappiness that characterize the human condition. It is likely that you, too, have never read anything like what follows. Guy suggests that the best way for the reader to approach this extraordinary material is to read the entire chapter through once, without stopping, so as to get the broad overview; and then read it a second time, slowly, to absorb its full meaning. To help lay the groundwork for what promises to be an amazing discovery about the secret nature of the intimate enemy, let me tell you about a personal experience of mine.—E.B.D.*

When I was still in my early teens, I read a book that had a tremendous influence on me. It was *Pride and Prejudice* by Jane Austen. From the moment I read its opening pages, I knew that I wanted to be the heroine of the novel, Elizabeth Bennet. Her flair and wit, her intelligence, and her ability to win the proud yet noble Mr. Darcy formed my ideal of the feminine character. During those early years, I must have read the book half a dozen times. Of course, as my life unfolded, the experiences I had were very different from those in the novel. I did not become Elizabeth Bennet, and eventually her image was relegated to the far reaches of my memory.

Many years later, the BBC produced a six-part dramatization of *Pride and Prejudice*. I bought the videos and spent two evenings immersed in a world I had first visited as an impressionable teenager. It was marvelous, but the best was yet to come—the startling insight I received later on that second night, after the videos had been rewound and put away. I was sitting in my favorite chair, finishing some tea, not really thinking about anything in particular, when I became aware of certain old familiar stirrings. A kind of melancholy descended upon me. Having been a student of myself for some time, I immediately became curious about what was going on and tried to track back the source of those feelings. It was then that I realized, with a shock, that I had become once again that same self I knew and had been when I was young and hoping for a heroine's life! In that instant of self-seeing it was clear that time was just an illusion. That person, with all her hopes and dreams and fears, was just as alive at that moment as she had been all those years before. She had never disappeared. She had remained hidden within me, just waiting for the right trigger to bring her forth. And now there was no doubt about it. This particular sentimental self that was first formed while reading that book so many years before was fully present in me, in charge of my emotions and running my thoughts!

"Now, wait a minute," you're saying. "Are you implying that there are different people inside of you, and that they take turns being in control?"

Yes! That's exactly what I'm saying, although it's important we don't get too far ahead of our lesson. Nevertheless, even though the idea may seem strange to you, this undetected multiplicity of selves is true about all of us. You can prove this finding for yourself. In fact, if you want to find real freedom, you must see the truth of this. The following paragraph lends some welcome light.

Haven't you ever gone to a store and bought something on impulse that you felt you just had to have? Then, when you got home, you couldn't imagine what had possessed you and you didn't want the thing at all! Real estate agents are familiar with this phenomenon. They even have a name for it: buyer's remorse. It's the same with our feelings about other people. We believe we are in love with someone on Monday. By Tuesday, they do nothing but annoy us. Then on Wednesday we are in love again! My closet is full of clothes that somebody else must have bought, because every time I look for something to wear, I can't find anything I like. I know you can come up with more examples for yourself. We like to think of ourselves as consistent people, but when we examine ourselves closely, we see that in fact we are moved around *within* ourselves, shifting from one self to another, as it were, more easily than the wind changes direction before an approaching storm.

In my own story about reliving a youthful experience after seeing a movie, a certain self that had lived within me since I was fourteen years old came right back to life when the conditions needed for its return came accidentally into place. For the few minutes that it was in charge, I experienced that same breathless excitement I felt when my whole life was still ahead of me; daring to hope of new tomorrows where fate, in cooperation with my plans, would lead me to *my* knight in shining armor.

A Startling Revelation that Brings True Success

Understanding that we are a multiplicity of selves is critical to recognizing, and ultimately defeating, the intimate enemy. During a small gathering of students Guy told two special stories to illustrate this extraordinary truth about ourselves.

The first story concerned the sinking of the Titanic and the behavior of the people caught up in the tragedy. When the "unsinkable" ocean liner struck an iceberg on its maiden voyage, the ship did not carry enough life rafts to save everyone on board. As this terrible truth became evident, panic spread throughout the entire ship and crew. While some of the passengers and ship's crew were able to maintain their composure, many others became hysterical, losing control of even the most elementary civilized behavior. In one scene from the movie made about this disaster, "A Night to Remember," in response to seeing everyone falling apart, a ship's steward called out to the terrified throng, "Take charge of yourselves!"

The point that Guy wished to make is that everyone who hears the phrase "Take charge of yourselves" knows exactly what it means.

Even without such stirring films as a reminder, all of us sense that, like the unlucky souls aboard *any* sinking ship, there is more than one person inside of us. One is screaming and pushing with absolutely no concern about who it has to hurt in order to save itself, while another knows that behavior of that kind betrays the decorum that civilized people are supposed to exhibit. To take charge of yourself is to remember that the qualities of courage, decency, and civility should prevail. When these qualities do not direct the individual and the terror-stricken child within wins out, it proves that, given the right conditions, each person's self-picture of being strong and in charge of himself is no more than a self-flattering, self-created image; and calling on an image to hold you together in tough times is like hoping a house of cards will protect you from a wind storm!

Guy's second story concerned an incident he had observed in a restaurant. On this particular occasion, Guy noticed three men dining at a nearby table who were busy gossiping and bragging about themselves. One of the men, who did his best to monopolize the conversation, boasted about how well his life was going. When the waiter asked if he wanted to order a drink, he claimed self-righteously to his friends that he had overcome his drinking problem and did not drink anymore.

After the meal was over, two of the men left, leaving behind the one who had been doing most of the talking. Within a few minutes a fourth man entered and joined the first, who now seemed to undergo a drastic change. This man, who only moments before had seemed so care-free, now proceeded to sadly relate some disturbing events from his past. And as he continued to talk over his difficulties, this same man who earlier that evening had proclaimed to the first group that he no longer drank, now ordered several drinks! It was as though he had no memory of who he had been only moments earlier. He had actually become a different person in the span of less than five minutes.

Guy explained that both of these stories point out an extremely important, but virtually unnoticed, characteristic of human beings and their psychology. *None of us is a singular, whole person.* Rather, each of us is a plurality, made up of many selves, but convinced we are a singularity. At any moment a different self can take the stage, and while it reigns it believes fully that it is the actual, complete person. But in fact, none of these selves is real. Each is no more than the creation of a temporary conjunction of conditions, and for this reason Guy has coined the phrase "Temporary Person in Charge," or TPIC (pronounced Tip´-ick), to describe them. From one minute to the next our values and desires can change, depending on which TPIC is in control.

A multitude of these Temporary Persons in Charge, or TPICs, lives within every one of us. They are, in a sense, the eyes through which we see the world and the thoughts that interpret it, which brings us to a very important point. This thought nature of a thousand selves has each of us unknowingly divided into a thousand different conflicting people. As each of these secret selves tries to prove it's permanent and real, it necessarily comes into conflict with other contradictory TPICs. Yet, each TPIC remains ignorant of the existence of the others. As a result, the division within our Self becomes deeper and gives rise to more unconscious discomfort. We've met these TPICs many times already in this book. They hold onto us in the form of hitchhiking negative spirits, and they are the thought-based soldiers who wage the war within us over the possession of countries that have no existence outside of our own imagination.

It is very important that we see clearly that our false nature is a multiplicity that only *believes* itself to be a singularity. This most vital spiritual discovery has gone unseen for good reason. As each TPIC comes to the forefront of our consciousness, it brings with it what amounts to its own complete history in the form of distinct memories and their requisite emotions. We take these thoughts and feelings as our own, identifying completely with that self to which they belong. Mathematician and author P.D. Ouspensky further explains this unsuspected psychic condition:

> *Man has no permanent and unchangeable I.* Every thought, every mood, every desire, every sensation says "I." And in each case it seems to be taken for granted that this I belongs to the Whole, to the whole man, and that a thought, a desire, or an aversion is expressed by this Whole.

To help understand these unusual internal workings, Vernon Howard once suggested to his students that they imagine a metal tube filled with hundreds of marbles of different colors. Further, the only way to see inside the tube is through a small window near the tube's center that is just large enough to reveal one marble at a time. Perhaps in one moment a yellow marble shows. Anyone looking through the tiny window who does not understand about the hundreds of marbles inside might assume that the inside of the tube is all yellow. Later, the tube is shaken, meaning that life changes, as it always does and must, and a green marble pops into the window slot. Now anyone looking at the tube might assume the inside of the tube is green. However, both of those conclusions, based on only partial knowledge, would be wrong.

In the same way, when we think about ourselves we believe that the thoughts we see and the self they belong to in that instant are the complete story. However, by stepping back from ourselves just for a moment, we can see more about ourselves than any such self-defining thoughts may tell. For one small example, the "ambitious" me, with all its plans and expectations has, in its isolated moment, no knowledge of that "hopeless" me who often fears the future, and which can appear at any time. Try to see the truth of this.

As the tube of our false selves is naturally shaken by ever-changing events, new personalities appear. And each one feels as though it is, and has always been, our present self. This may be difficult to grasp about ourselves for now, but in other areas of our lives it's more than evident. So, let's look there.

We're often deceived when we look at other people and believe in whatever self they present at any moment. That's why we're shocked when the person we always thought was a "sweet baby blue" marble suddenly turns into an "angry red" one. We quickly make excuses to explain the discrepancy. "Something just came over him," we say. "It will never happen again." But it does happen again, because given the right cue, that TPIC *will* reappear. The truth of this fact is more than self-evident in our experience both with others . . . and ourselves.

As we become newly aware that in our unawakened state we live in and from a multiplicity of diverse selves, that very awareness begins to bring about the end to all these temporary persons who take charge of our lives. As the whirling, changing selves begin to fade, which they must do in the light of our growing awareness of them, something real, something peaceful, begins to reveal itself to us *from within us*. As we come to live from our emerging, True, Singular Self, there are no more false soldiers being unconsciously created to fight imaginary battles, and then . . . *the inner war is won through its very disappearance.*

The Internal Working of the Intimate Enemy

Now that we have some understanding of these temporary personalities that act in our name from moment to moment, we can go a step deeper to examine their source.

Each one of us, from the moment we're born, begins to have experiences that take part in molding our

developing character. Psychologists who call themselves behaviorists refer to this process as conditioning.
They believe that our experiences with reward and
punishment completely determine our developing personality, including our values, beliefs, and emotional
reactions. Other psychologists believe that certain
inborn physiological factors, such as excitability, mod-
ify our reactions to experiences. They believe that this
inborn temperament has an important effect on the
personality that emerges.

From the point of view of the deeper psychological
studies that we are pursuing here, what the behaviorists
and temperament psychologists provide is a description
of the conglomeration of traits and responses that sit at
the surface of each individual's personality. These elements of the personality have developed by chance and
in no particular order. They are changeable and fragmentary, and involve self-pictures that vary from circumstance
to circumstance. These elements that have no permanent
reality make up what many spiritual scientists call the
"false nature."

For the majority of people who never look beyond the
surface of their lives, the reactions of these false, con-
structed selves are all they ever know about themselves.
They respond mechanically to events without ever questioning their responses, or how those responses change
from moment to moment. These men and women never
question the confusion and heartache that comes with trying to live a real, consistent life, while being whipsawed by

this ever-changing false nature. Rarely, if ever, do these people wonder why they so often feel threatened and defensive without bringing others into the picture as being the cause. Yet the real sorrow in all of this isn't in the kind of life these individuals are resigned to, but in the fact that they unknowingly deny themselves a true life through their unquestioned false assumptions about themselves. We must, and can, learn to be different. The encouraging facts that follow point the way.

Somewhere, beneath all the added-on characteristics at the surface of the personality, a Real Self is waiting to emerge. It is that "still small" part of us, an undivided self that, by and in its very own wholeness, is capable of observing the ever-changing kaleidoscope of the false nature . . . and that which, in seeing the false self—in the light of its own wholly awakened state—also sees that the pains and problems of this much-separated self are as unreal and unnecessary to Real Life as is the lesser-self itself. But it would be getting ahead of our story to go into this too deeply here. For now, it is only necessary to understand that we each have a false nature that is presently acting as an intermediary between who we really are and the world around us. It is this same false nature that both creates and places us on the psychological battlefield, and that prevents us from directly experiencing life from our Higher, Real Selves. This false nature *is* the intimate enemy, and its *only* power over each of us is in what we don't as yet understand about it, which means it is soon to be powerless!

Meet the Temporary Person
in Charge of You

As we have seen, we each have, and operate from, a false
nature that is a jumble of our memories, conditioning,
and some temperamental qualities. It is this unsuspected
false nature that meets the world each day, responding to
and interpreting each and every one of life's fluctuations.
It is very important for us to begin to understand that of
themselves these ever-changing conditions in life are neutral, but the false nature imposes its own meaning on all
these life changes; labeling and defining them so much so
that the event you see unfolding before you is really nothing more than a circumstantial creation of the false self.
We can clear up any confusion you may have about this
last idea with a simple example.

   If you looked at the world through green lenses, everything you saw would be tinted green. Similarly, the false
nature, which is a product of our past, can only see the
flow of present events through the lenses of its experience. It recognizes present situations by considering the
past, and once it's clear on what's happening, out pops a
TPIC to take charge of that situation. The TPIC, a custom
creation of the false self, is put into action to safely steer
the individual through this circumstance, but remember:
the circumstance under consideration, whatever it may
be, is itself created by an interpretation of the real event
by the false nature. This last insight is an important point
for study. Reread it several times until its full meaning is
revealed to you. To the unaware person, the event may
feel new and so may his or her response, but in fact, both

are based on the past. Rarely, if ever, do we see things as they really are, but only through an interpretation of them. We rarely respond spontaneously, but mostly as we have done before. All forms of adaptive behavior learned to help free us in the present moment still leave us acting out of the false prison of the past. No wonder we find ourselves caught up in the same kinds of situations again and again, and nothing ever seems to be resolved in a new way.

To make matters worse, each time a new challenge seems to come before us, yet another new TPIC pops up to handle it. As a result, from one moment to the next our behavior and our plans change, causing us to run through a gamut of emotions and thoughts within a short period of time. This emotional roller coaster ride can leave us drained and confused. Let's look at an example of how a series of events can lead to the emergence of a series of very different selves.

You're in your office, thinking about what you're going to order for lunch, when a co-worker comes in and tells you that a mistake was found in a report you had submitted a week before. The serious expression on her face and the word "mistake" immediately give rise to a conditioned response of fear. As the false nature responds in this way, a temporary personality, a TPIC, pops up to interpret that emotional reaction and to take charge of the condition that the fear has defined. The co-worker's statement about a mistake being made, which in itself had no necessary emotional meaning for you, becomes an "event," in this case, a threatening one. The TPIC that pops up starts taking what it sees as the appropriate defensive action. It

starts justifying itself, which includes looking for someone else to blame for the error. It quickly focuses on your
boss, who had pressured you to get that report in early.
Now an angry TPIC pops up, resenting this boss who
always makes your life so difficult and never gives you
credit for anything. You start thinking about how you
would like to get revenge on this person by revealing to
other people some unflattering things you suspect about
him. As this TPIC revels in scenes of embarrassing your
boss, it is blissfully unaware that what it sees as a tri-
umphant solution has nothing to do with resolving the
original "problem," which was the error in the report.

At this point, who should appear at your door but the
very boss you have just been humiliating in your mind.
You are no longer the self-righteous, aggrieved victim, for
the changing circumstance has caused a new TPIC to pop
up who perhaps may start to fawn before this character
who signs your paycheck. Now, to your delight, you realize that he has come to praise you. The smile on his face
and the words "great job" fill you with pleasure and confidence.

Yet again, and still undetected, a new TPIC steps forward to remind you of your intention to invite your boss
to your home for dinner. This seems perfectly reasonable
to you, and you see no conflict with the self of just a few
moments before who wanted to embarrass, rather than
entertain, the gentleman. As the boss leaves, you feel
pleased with yourself and let your imagination roam free,
contemplating how you will spend the raise you're now
expecting. This contented TPIC has no memory of the

nervous, displaced-feeling TPIC of only a moment before. It now thinks that *it* is the singular self, that *it* is the real you. Nothing could be further from the truth.

We have had it shown to us in this chapter that from moment to moment, we bounce back and forth from one temporary personality to another. One is happy, and one is depressed. One is excited, and one is bored. Like a leaf in the wind, our mood and outlook are blown one way and another, with no central self in control. At each moment, we believe fully in each temporary self; as it thinks, so do we. We pay dearly for this misunderstanding, for we unconsciously rely on these TPICs to deal with and solve the many problems that we face every day. Of course, we don't see these ever-shifting selves as the temporary personalities they really are. We believe that each one, as it takes control, is who we really are.

Now, here's another fascinating higher insight for your self-study. Each TPIC feels capable of handling whatever the new challenge may be, because it believes that it is independent of the condition it tries to control. But it is not. In reality, this temporary self now striving to call the shots for you didn't even exist until the condition in question made its appearance before your mind's eye. And here's a key concept to grasp: that condition it "sees"— whatever it may be—is itself only a conditioned response, a mechanical mental or emotional reaction of the false self in the form of either resisting or embracing the naturally changing circumstances.

These last few findings are vital to understanding our developing study, because within them is hidden another

powerful inner discovery vital for our victory over the
intimate enemy.

Every action the TPIC takes to free itself of any troubling situation secretly confirms its initial mistaken interpretation that created that situation. This unconscious
confirmation process secretly serves the false self in an
unsuspected and sinister way. If the situation it sees
looming ahead is real, then so must be that growing sense
of self that you have no choice but to be its victim. For
example, the man who blames his boss for the frustration
he feels unconsciously perpetuates his belief that he is,
and must remain, someone who can only feel good about
his work as long as others pat him on the back. This man
is an unconscious victim of his own perception, and the
punishment he feels can't change until he changes the
way he sees life.

Clearly, the TPIC cannot fix the situation that created
it, and that it now sees as a problem, any more than a
misshapen reflection in a funhouse mirror can straighten
the glass to "save" the person being reflected, which leads
us to another important consideration in our investigation of the intimate enemy. Not only is the TPIC unable
to correct any condition that calls it into temporary existence, but in order for the TPIC to perpetuate itself,
which it wants to do, this self-styled false self actually
requires the continuation of the event that gave rise to it!

Yes, the TPIC may put on a show of solving the problem, but its efforts can never be successful because it
always sees the cause of the problem in the external
event. All its efforts in that direction must fail because the

true cause lies within the false self and its self-imposed definition of the event. All its efforts to solve the external problem, as it defines it, simply keeps itself, and the problem, going. Can you see how this new finding sheds light on the real root of our ever-recurring painful patterns in life? And how these unconscious patterns serve the goal of the TPIC, which is to maintain itself? While on the opposite side, when a pleasurable situation presents itself, the TPIC believes it has the ability to keep it going forever. However, that TPIC was created in response to conditions that it has no power to control. When those conditions change, so does that TPIC, and the happy self gives way to a disappointed one.

Each new occurrence in life gives rise to another TPIC, and as each new TPIC pops into the driver's seat, it brings with it a full explanation of who we are and what we must do to steer ourselves straight. These explanations appear so logical to us we are able to ignore any faint echoes from an old TPIC that may conflict with what the current self is saying. Each new TPIC has virtually absolute authority, for even though we may sense at times that we are not really in control of our lives, we refuse to investigate, and instead throw in all our forces with whatever TPIC reigns at the moment. Should we come right up against behavior that conflicts with our self-image, even then we can keep up our belief that we live from a central self. We simply proclaim we don't know what came over us; we blame the situation or the other person for making us act a certain way; or we claim to hate that TPIC (perhaps a bad habit or some compulsive behavior) and proclaim that the "real me" will fight it. No matter what happens, the invisible superstructure of the TPICs remains intact.

Each TPIC is accompanied by a specialized kind of psychic program that supports it, complete with memories, preferences, and beliefs. That program enables it to function and to use everything that occurs to prove that it is what it thinks and feels itself to be. For example, when you're feeling unhappy, and someone comes along who disturbs you further, the TPIC produces from memory a complete list of past insults to explain why that person has always been a torment to you. In a flash, the facts are gathered and distorted to support the belief, and the TPIC's emotional state confirms it.

Here's another amazing point to ponder and to help you break away from the false authority of the TPICs. Each new TPIC can only be in charge of your life for as long as the condition that brought it into existence continues. In other words, a TPIC has no staying power because it is formed by the conjunction of an external cue and a mechanical internal reaction. Let's see how this is true.

Suppose, for example, the doctor's scale reports a five-pound weight gain. The false nature experiences guilt and fear that it will no longer be considered attractive. A TPIC pops up to take charge of the situation, and vows to go on a diet and avoid temptation at all costs, but when the external condition changes, a new response is evoked. As the reaction that created that TPIC fades, so does that TPIC. A new reaction to a new condition now gives rise to a new TPIC. The old TPIC is forgotten because the very thing that created it is gone. So, when a friend suggests trying a new Mexican restaurant that just opened, you agree without hesitation. Now, a fun-loving, hungry TPIC comes into play, and the morning's resolution is either forgotten or explained away. The TPIC in control can, and does, switch in an unseen instant. This shift in selves happens so quickly and smoothly that the person of one moment eagerly anticipating the meal never sees the conflict with the dieter of a moment before. Remember the man at the restaurant who "gave up" drinking?

How Awakened Awareness
Leads to Victory

The reason we've never noticed that we are inhabited self, by self, by self, is because we have never been aware of their inner transitions. The nature we presently live from is designed to keep us in the dark and serve these fictitious selves, not for learning to see them. As we are now, we wholly become each TPIC as it takes over. Revealing these truths about the changing TPICs has always been the focus of real spiritual studies. Christ called this false self "the first," as in, "the first shall be last." The Sufis refer to the "commanding self." Western psychology refers to it as the ego, the persona, or the roles we play. No matter how these approaches discuss the TPIC, there is one dominating fact: the TPIC *is not the real you!* This means you no longer need struggle with any sinking feeling you have about your life. Your capacity for self-awareness is greater than any limitation created by undetected TPICs. As you begin to wield this mighty weapon of new self-awareness, as you let the Light fight for you, not only do the TPICs lose their power to misguide you, but they begin to disappear altogether! This is what we're after.

As Guy explains in *The Secret of Letting Go:* "Freedom from any conflict, captivity, or punishing condition, must be proceeded by your awareness of the disturbance." The Roman philosopher Marcus Aurelius supports this finding while looking at it from another angle. He writes: "Those who do not observe the movements of their own minds must of necessity be unhappy." In other words, we can't be free of any self-limitation until we recognize it for what it really is. Presently, we believe the TPICs are real, and that their battles with life are necessary to protect us from pain. We don't see that the pain we feel is due to our identification with these artificial identities, and that we can't be free of what is punishing us as long as we take it for our friend. However, as we start to see what it is that is really punishing us, we also begin to see that we had the power to be free all the time!

Try something right now that will put you in a different relationship with life by increasing your self-awareness. While lifting your hand before you, simply be aware of it. Feel its weight and movement. Now, become aware of yourself being aware of your hand. Can you feel how this puts you in a different relationship with everything around you, how it puts you into a different relationship with yourself? You now see that in the first instance, before this new awareness was added to the picture, there was no discernible difference between you and the moment of moving your hand around. In the second instance, however, *with* your heightened awareness a part of your actions, you can say, "I am aware of myself in the situation." And this new self-awareness puts *you* in command.

You can have this same kind of higher relationship—this same command—over your own false nature and its many TPICs. Here's how to begin. Each time you can become aware of any TPIC, and "see" yourself being aware of it, it can no longer remain in unconscious control of you. This state of self-seeing is the beginning of real self-command—but this is only the start! Let the following sentence reveal to you something about yourself beyond thought: your very awareness of yourself is a special kind of proof that the awareness exists beyond the self it is aware of. This self-discovery produces something that is at the heart of spiritual transformation: the first stages of being able to consciously separate yourself from any troubling TPIC.

In fact, the only way the intimate enemy, and the many TPICs arising from it, can ever be overcome is by calling upon this true intelligence inherent in higher awareness of ourselves. TPICs are not intelligent of themselves because, as products of thought, they are by nature fragmented and temporary creations. But what is within us, what is capable of observing each TPIC as it arises, is Timeless and True. As we work to stay aware of each TPIC, this awareness puts us in charge of these ever-changing surface selves and begins to produce the peace we've been seeking; a deep sense of contentment and confidence comes to us that no TPIC can ever know.

Our new and higher knowledge of the TPIC is our primary defense against being dragged into the self-compromising emotions and behavior it demands. To help us gain this self-knowledge, Guy gave us the following exercise:

Take a piece of paper and place at the top the heading, "Temporary Selves For Self-Study." Then, as you learn to observe yourself, write down each personality that you recognize taking charge of your life. Soon, you'll have a long list of different selves that take turns on center stage. Of special educational value is to make conscious note of the opposite selves that may be in control at different times. As you proceed with this special self-study, you will become more aware of the temporary nature of each TPIC, and, with time, you will not believe as strongly in any of them, knowing that its opposite is always ready to come forth and displace it. As your awareness grows of how each TPIC is actually not a part of the solution, but a secret extension of the problem, you'll start to believe in all of them less and less. Now, you are on your way to winning the war within yourself!

The exercise above is designed to help us see all of the contradictions in our own consciousness along with their resulting punishment. We must get glimpses of the jumble of selves that rule us so we can begin to differentiate what is real from what is only a product of a confused mind. Real self-change and the victory it brings with it means only to drop our belief in that which has never been real in the first place. Then the Higher Self, which has always been there, begins to take its rightful place in directing our lives. Happiness is always close at hand, but this real self-change has a real cost.

An ancient scripture says, "When you see the angel of death approaching there is great fear. But when he finally arrives, there is bliss." One part of the secret meaning in this statement is that as the false self feels that it is losing its power and realizes that you intend for it to lose its life, it brings out its big guns: fear. But you need not and you must not be turned away. This false nature knows it must keep control of your life so that it can continue to have its own un-life. But as it passes away, which it must if you persist with your self-studies, you soon see that all the fear was unnecessary, because that which is dying within you *was never real to begin with*. Then there is only that contentment and effortless self-command that is the natural fruit of living from our own Higher Nature.

To hasten this moment of transcending what you have always taken to be yourself, you must go beyond your usual thinking. You must be willing to meet life with your eyes open in the sense of *seeing* things as they are instead of listening to the TPICs *tell you* what you see. This specialized shift in your psychology must be purposely developed. Higher self-awareness is a volitional act.

At first, working to meet life without your usual interpretations and reactions may actually seem to add to your confusion. It may even feel that you're worse off than ever. Nevertheless, persist! This confusion is just a trick of the TPIC. Not only are you in a wonderful place to start winning the war within yourself, it's the *only* place to make a new beginning: letting the old, stale reactor die a little each day, so that we can experience real life as it is and enjoy what it brings with it.

As we grow in this New Life we learn real compassion for ourselves and for everyone else struggling under the fleeting control of a thousand TPICs. And as we are gradually carried beyond the superficiality of our present lives, we are astounded at the limited view that once directed our every thought and deed. Reality itself takes control of our lives. Gone forever is that sense of self that is troubled. Now we know that our only enemy in life was that false perception that there was an enemy in the first place.

Special Summary

If we'll learn to live without telling ourself who we are—and without knowing what to do about our pain—the day will arrive when we'll have seen so much about what's hurting us, we just won't look to it anymore for who we are.

—Guy Finley
The Secret Way of Wonder

5

> *You have a right not to be negative.*
>
> — Maurice Nicoll

BREAK FREE OF ALL PAINFUL PATTERNS

Perhaps you've noticed this: unhappiness is not uncommon these days. And if sad conditions aren't bad enough in themselves, it seems to take less and less to make us feel this way. We go to the store and see that prices have risen. Our rosebushes fail to thrive. That hoped-for phone call never rings in. So common, and so frequent, in fact, are these twinges of pain, both large and small, that we have come to accept their troubling presence within us as being a natural part of daily life; and life itself seems to support our conclusion.

Seemingly well-meaning people tell us, "You've got to take the good with the bad." Or, we tell ourselves in times of trial, "If it weren't for my sorrow, I would never really enjoy my happy times!" The truth is, these statements are nothing more than propaganda; they are partially truthful

87

ideas all mixed up into false self-notions by the intimate enemy in order to extend its base of unquestioned authority to perpetuate heartache. So far, it and its mangled message have succeeded in both directing and dominating our lives. Fortunately, this unhappy cycle of self, as well as the suffering its level enables, can be ended. But breaking out of painful patterns must begin with bringing new knowledge into the way we've been thinking toward our old problems. So, allow the new knowledge in this next study section to start freeing you.

Make the Shadows in Your Life Disappear

All of us already know that things are not always what they seem. On the other hand, what is virtually unknown is that many problems that appear at first to be insurmountable only seem that way to us because of the degree of pain we feel when considering our unwanted condition. Our new studies, however, clearly show that most of our conclusions concerning our "impossible" conditions are, in fact, nothing more than a powerful misperception cast upon us by the TPIC of the moment. So it is that we come to a great moment in our search for self-liberation: seeing through our own misperception of reality is the same as seeing that whatever suffering it brought with it is no more than an illusion. Our psychological suffering is not the power we have taken it to be, because *it is not based in reality*.

During one rainy Sunday meeting, Guy shared with us an illustration that sheds new light on the pain we feel and reveals why it is unnecessary. Do you remember when you were a child and you lay in bed at night, afraid of the strange figures that danced menacingly along your wall? Perhaps you asked your father to leave a light on for you because you were afraid of the monsters that came out in the dark. Your father may have laughed comfortingly, and against your protests, made you get out of bed to look outside the window. There you saw a branch blowing in the wind, and looking back at the wall, realized, for yourself, that the "monster" you were so afraid of was nothing more than a shadow. Your child's mind now understood, although it might not have been able to put it into words, that the shadow had no substance of its own, but was merely an effect. It disappeared when the light came on because the conditions necessary for its appearance no longer held. The shadow itself had no power to do you harm. It was only your attribution of power to the shadow that put the fear of it into you. Now let's see what this simple but extraordinary discovery can do for us if we carefully apply its lesson to those psychic shadows we call our suffering.

In the last chapter we learned that with each occurrence in our lives, the false nature unconsciously and automatically responds by calling up a TPIC to interpret and deal with this event. It could be said that in each of these moments the TPIC sheds *its* light of understanding on the event. Even a small amount of honest self-reflection reveals these inner workings. For instance, when the false nature feels itself threatened or thwarted, an aggressive or negative TPIC comes forward, seeing everything in a fearful, dark light. This self then supports its view by gathering additional thoughts about "the event." These thoughts might relive the past that led up to the event, or anticipate possible future consequences. As each potential problem grows in magnitude as a result of our unconscious attention to it, our negative emotional response grows stronger. Each and all of these subsequent negativities are nothing more than the shadows cast by the first TPIC's false light. However, unaware of their real cause, we fear the pictures they paint in the same way as the child feared the shadows on the wall. Fortunately, just as a strong overhead light banishes shadows from a physical wall, the light of Truth has the power to banish all inner shadows and the suffering which, in turn, shadows them.

An example will explain. Perhaps a woman discovers that she has been betrayed by a friend. One TPIC that pops up to deal with this situation is outraged. It builds a strong case against the betrayer and revels in scenes of revenge. In no time it gives way to another TPIC that feels hurt, bemoaning its fate by "the fact" that no one can be trusted. Piece by piece it paints a picture of a dark, lonely world where everyone is a potential enemy. Or perhaps still a third TPIC remembers happy scenes of their past friendship, and despairs over their loss. No doubt the pain this woman experiences in the hands of each of these TPICs is genuine; but the cause, in each case, is only a shadow on the wall! Let's see how this can be true.

Suppose this woman has been working with the life-healing principles we're in the process of learning. Within this individual a developing higher awareness no longer just unconsciously accepts these changeable TPICs and embraces *their* conclusions. Instead, she chooses in favor of wanting to see the truth of her situation, a view that reveals to her the fact that the host of vicious voices she hears in her head are themselves the pain of the betrayal she's feeling. Proceeding from this new understanding of herself she sees that while her friend's betrayal proves she must reevaluate their relationship, the act of someone having betrayed her is not the source of her stress. She sees clearly that both the real problem she faces and its punishment are what they are because of her unconscious fear of being betrayed by anyone. She also sees that the reason she so fears this betrayal is because, up until this point, she had unconsciously believed that other people's opinions of her had the power to build or diminish her. Now, she knows this idea, and any part of herself that promotes it, is the only betrayer—the invisible intimate enemy. Even more importantly, she now knows that the false self in her that fears betrayal is no more real than the weak self that popped up in her former friend causing her to commit the betrayal. She begins to understand that the whole suffering scene is part of the confused world of TPICs that wander through life, hurting and being hurt. And in proportion to her new understanding also grows within her the wish to no longer live in their troubled world. She may not know it yet, but this wish itself belongs to another part of herself that is already connected to something timeless and all powerful; a True Self that can help her use the betrayals of this world as a springboard to leap above and beyond them to a higher world where fear simply doesn't exist. Yes, there is a way out, and a Self within you that knows the way.

Discover the New You in a New View

When we're in pain most of us will do whatever seems necessary to bring relief. Almost any behavior can be justified when pain pushes us far enough, but our new perspective on mental and emotional pain shows us we need not, and must not, handle it as we've always been directed to in the past. What we do need is to grow in our understanding of it. When we shine the light of this new understanding into any situation, we no longer produce shadows to fear. And without fear we are free. Certainly, conditions may present themselves that we must deal with in a practical way, but there are no battles to fight. Again, the fearful shadows created by the intimate enemy disappear in the light of higher awareness. Remember: your True Self doesn't win in life by overpowering problems, but by revealing they never really existed as you once believed they did.

Look at what this discovery does for us: we've always believed there weren't too many choices for us outside of remaining unwilling victims of unhappy conditions that were too much for us. Now we have seen that the Truth can take us out of any unhappy condition because it knows that psychological suffering is based only on our mistaken ideas about ourselves. This can be difficult to accept. Tell some people that their mental or emotional suffering has no real basis and their response will be to start suffering right before your eyes, justifying their inflamed state by claiming that in such circumstances as the one they cite, there is no alternative but this—their pain.

Let's set the record straight. There are many things that have happened and that are happening in this world that are, at best, difficult to deal with. There's no question about it: human beings often do awful things to each other. Certainly, compassion is in terribly short supply. But the key point for our inner work is that events—*in themselves*—do not have the power to make us suffer. It is our reaction that throws us, unaware, into the world of our unenlightened selves. Where these spirits rule, so does suffering. The proof of this crucial finding, that events themselves are not the source of our pains, can be found in the many examples throughout history. In every age there have been those people who have overcome highly challenging events to emerge not only stronger but with a new wisdom that can never be made to suffer again in the same old way. A real-life story illustrates this truth.

Some years ago, a brilliant young athlete was injured in an accident that left him paralyzed. Instead of falling into despair, he went on to help other young people who were similarly injured to overcome their own sense of loss. When he was interviewed about how the accident had changed his life and about the work he was now doing, he made some very revealing comments. He said that as a result of his accident his life had taken on an entirely new dimension that he never would have been able to foresee. His life-shattering experiences had so enriched him that, even if given a choice, he wouldn't change anything that had happened.

This young man chose to learn the life-elevating lesson in the event, rather than be defeated by it. Because of that, he came to realize that his True Self is not tied to his physical body or to competitive success. His seeming loss at the level of this life opened the door to a spiritual awakening that filled him with greater meaning than any man-made trophy ever could. Although to the eyes of the world he had become more limited, in fact his universe had expanded to support a life of freedom beyond anything he could have hoped for in his former state. An event that could have been devastating to someone who responded mechanically, or who believed in the necessity of suffering, became a life-ennobling event for someone who was willing to let himself be shown his own life in a new way. An old Arabic saying suggests the secret behind this triumph: The nature of rain is the same, but it makes thorns grow in the marshes and flowers in the gardens.

In his inspiring book *Man's Search for Meaning*, Viktor Frankl describes his experiences as a prisoner in a Nazi death camp. While many became embittered and hardened in their captivity, some were able to transcend even those horrifying circumstances to develop a relationship with a higher power. No longer tied to the meanness and cruelty of the world in which they found themselves physically, they achieved a spiritual understanding that lifted their lives far beyond the reach of man's inhumanity to man. Such self-transformation may seem incomprehensible to those who take anger at the world's injustice as their right. Yet, when each of us realizes that we're not participating in the full spectrum of life due to our conditioned misperception of it, then we'll start appreciating all of life's events—good and bad—and we'll seek the continuing discovery of our True Selves *within* all events rather than trying to protect ourselves *from* them. The difference in these two life paths is the difference between finding out that life already has its own higher purpose for you, or struggling your whole life to prove your own purpose.

Yes, the first path that leads to the Higher Life is more difficult in the beginning. It demands rather than just accepting our heartaches that we investigate them in order to come upon their real source, for only here can they be ended forever. Instead of that downward slide into yourself called suffering, this first path provides definite steps up and out of yourself. So, let's take another of these upward-leading steps toward our True Self.

As difficult as it may be, *we must begin to doubt our own suffering.* This new action may seem impossible at first because our pain can feel so real. But, if we'll put ourselves on the side of wanting and working to see what is the actual truth of our situation, our gradually deepening perception will show us how to see through that suffering straight to the heart of its shadowy cause. For example, when we fight with the person we blame for our discomfort, all we do is increase our anguish which, in turn, strengthens our belief in that person as being our punisher. If instead we turn our attention back on ourselves, we can start to question this habitual view of our situation. Now, instead of just accepting stock answers as to why we must ache, we can ask new questions about the necessity of that conflict. For instance, what is it about us that is vulnerable to being hurt by anything someone else does? With just this one question in mind, that person's action is no longer the issue. The issue is what is happening within us.

To further focus on this important part of our study, let's look at two common forms of suffering to reveal how they are based in our own misperception. First we'll examine the unsuspected pain we all feel over the impermanent nature of life. Then we will look at the pain we unconsciously bear when living under the weight of life's false responsibilities.

Shed New Light on the Pain of Impermanence

We all want the comfort of knowing that there are things we can count on, that there is something in this life *permanent*. Yet, everything seems to slip away from us; people, places, and events all change. And as they go so does our sense of security, leaving us once again seeking something to give us a permanent sense of well-being. There is a cure for this seemingly endless longing. It is a spiritual one. Something does exist that isn't temporary. Something is Permanent. But to find it, we first must lose our misplaced faith in those things that have always let us down in the past. To help us better understand this problem of impermanence, and why the pain surrounding it is so persistent, Guy provides us with an insight-filled illustration. It explains why we have so often been left floating adrift.

Suppose that an unsuspecting seventeenth-century sea captain sets sail on his trade route in a ship fitted with a false anchor. The anchor looks real and solid, but in fact is nothing more than steel pellets and salt shaped in a sand casting mold and covered with a thin binding coat of lead paint. When this anchor is dropped in the water, it is only a matter of time before the binding paint and salt dissolve, leaving the pellets to disperse. Nothing is left to hold the ship, which now drifts aimlessly onto the shoals. The sea captain's despair is the salvage crew's joy! It turns out, not coincidentally, that the owner of this salvage company also has another company that secretly sells these false anchors to unwary ship owners. If you don't see the connection yet with how the TPIC has been sinking your "ship," the following explanation tells all.

How many times have we thrown out a false psychological anchor that has been passed off on us as a solid one? With each one we thought that this time we would be safe in this job, this relationship, this new home, only to find ourselves eventually wrecked on some jagged reef. Even the anchor of anger, which seemed so justified, might have made us feel strongly solid for a while before it too melted away, leaving us empty, and perhaps a little embarrassed. And false anchors don't always lead us into negative situations. Sometimes things do seem to work out. Perhaps the relationship does last, but again, the comfort is impermanent. The longing for something more returns, and tells us that even our best relationship is not the answer to the emptiness inside. So, we throw out new anchors, so many that we never notice our recurring crashes on the shoals, because the idea of our next safe anchorage is ready to rescue us at a moment's notice. Is there any such thing as a permanent anchor that doesn't dissolve and cast us adrift?

A permanent anchor does exist, but before we can benefit from its steady hold we must break the cycle of suffering inherent in our unquestioned trust of—and hope for security in—our many false anchors. This brings us to a very important point to ponder. Let the depth of it fall into your wish for a still deeper understanding of all that it suggests.

There can never be a permanent anchor in this physical world of ours because the sea of time dissolves everything. Even we dissolve in the sea of time. This is not a fact to fear, but one to understand. Facts like these lead us to discover the one thing that isn't temporary, something right in the center of each of us that can't come unglued and is never blown off course.

Anchor Yourself to an Unsinkable Security

Something permanent exists above the present level of our life experience. We rarely feel the security of this True Anchor in our everyday lives where we seldom finish a line of action, or, for that matter, even a topic of discussion! Each new TPIC provides a new false anchor by telling us what we need to do to get over the feeling of drifting. The anchor feels solid at the time, but as conditions change, a new TPIC pops up. The TPIC throws out that anchor based on what it knows, which is just one more thing that cannot work because no TPIC, or its creation, can have any real permanence.

However, we need not continue to ache from these aimless actions. Deep within us, beyond all the TPICs, lies a true awareness that is a part of our genuine self.

This higher awareness is both bedded in Permanence and is itself part of that solid ground. At any moment we can actually see the TPIC in action, we are, in that split second of awareness, actually standing on this higher ground and in touch with something permanent within us. Guy gave us an exercise to encourage these special moments of self-awakening.

At least once each day try to connect even five minutes of your day. That is, for these five minutes *know* what you're doing the entire time, so that something in you remains aware of each changing thought and feeling but doesn't change with them—instead it watches them come and go. Instead of saying "I" to each TPIC in this special period of self-study, be there to say "Bye-Bye" as each leaves the stage of your consciousness.

Staying anchored in awareness of ourselves in this way is the beginning of the birth of our Authentic or True Self. This higher awareness of ourselves is both *in* the flow of what's going on, yet *outside* of the flow of time. It *cannot be dissolved.* In the beginning of our attempts to stay anchored within ourselves we'll find it difficult to remain newly aware for more than a few moments at a time. Even our failed attempts bring a new self-understanding that we could not have guessed at before.

One of our greatest lessons comes when we actually catch ourselves in the process of dropping an anchor that we think will supply us with a new sense of permanence, and then watch that anchor dissolve as things shift once more. We thought the relationship would make us feel right about ourselves, but soon we felt insecure again. Then, it was the money that offered a chance at happiness, but no matter how much we made, it was never enough. As we learn to watch this happening again and again, we begin to understand that our thoughts about ourselves, and what they tell us we need for security, have no substance themselves. So, bit by bit it dawns upon us: *we can't think ourselves into permanence.* We can see ourselves in the act of creating and then dropping a false anchor, however, and it is this Higher awareness, itself, that brings with it the real permanence we've been seeking. Although these moments of inner-magic don't last long, as it isn't in our power to will ourselves into lasting self-awareness, we always have the opportunity to catch ourselves again. This inner work of waking up and letting go, waking up and letting go, is like opening sails and catching fresh friendly winds over and over. Past troubled waters smooth out. Even new storms don't shake us the way they used to, for a new anchor begins to secure us in the permanent waters of Reality.

Now let's look at another mistaken notion people have that causes them to suffer needlessly: a false sense of responsibility.

How to Care for Yourself in a New Way

If you haven't noticed this yet about yourself, it's easy to see in others: we each seem to carry the weight of the world on our shoulders. The nature of this burden may change with age. When young, we feel the weight of having to choose a direction in life. As adults, we feel encumbered by all the perceived requirements of an active life:

trying to control events, win acceptance, maintain relationships, on and on, with each new self-shaped solution
for success only increasing our burden. Then, as we naturally mature and slow down, we often find ourselves feeling oppressed by the things left undone or mistakes made
along the way. In short, regardless of our age, we tend to
feel weighted down by what we perceive as our responsibility to create and live a "meaningful" life.

Each of us, to some extent, feels certain that we are
obligated to carry this weight. Our idea of shouldering it
is to work hard, struggling to appear important in the
eyes of others, as well as in our own. It's a wearisome task
with few real rewards, and since the only real pressure
we're under is self-imposed, the only relief we find is
when we get off of our own backs!

Surprisingly, most people recoil at the suggestion that
the weight they carry is in their own minds only. "I'm a
responsible person," they proclaim. "*That's* why I suffer. In
fact, my suffering is proof of just how responsible I am!"

All of us have heard such claims. We may even have
spoken these words, or at least felt these sentiments, ourselves. But our new studies speak otherwise. They reveal
that not only should we not suffer over whatever we have
assumed as our responsibility, but that our first real
responsibility is to see through all forms of self-created
suffering. Let's take a closer look into this contradictory
condition within ourselves.

To begin with, we want things to change. This wish, in
itself, is like believing that being anxious about whether
the sun rises or not will help it to do so. Life is change.

But we also want it to get better, which means to change according to our own notions of success. So, we try to control what happens, believing that the tension this causes between life and our ideas about it is what it means to feel responsible. There is something misplaced in this mixture of life and our longings that grows unseen. The reason we strain as we do to carry this daily load is because we believe it is what's required of us to create a real self.

However, for all our struggle, no permanent self appears; only a kind of peculiar suffering manifests itself again and again, giving us an unwanted sense that its permanence may be all there is to life. The only self that finds this sad state of affairs to its liking is the intimate enemy, because its idea of permanence means having something to struggle with permanently! When we try to change life in response to the prodding of this false self, the results are what Guy terms "self-formational."

All self-formational changes are awkward and temporary at best, because they are not rooted in reality. The struggle we undergo to bring them about is not only painful in itself, but causes additional suffering, as when our false sense of responsibility causes us not only to interfere with our own lives, but also with those of others around us. Wrongly believing that the way someone else behaves is our responsibility not only makes us suffer, but that person as well when we try to meddle with his or her life. Our growing awareness of our mistake causes us to become disenchanted with the self-formational approach to living, and we begin to seek the transformational life instead.

Break the Chains of False Responsibility

Wouldn't you like to just let go? To release once and for all that recurring feeling that you're just not making it? Or, how about the weight of fearing what others think of you? Your concern for the future? Wouldn't it be wonderful to just drop the burden of feeling responsible for the outcome of every event? Yes. It is possible to live this lightly.

As we recognize the futility of trying to force ourselves and our lives into what we think they should be, we also begin to understand that all of our suffering for what we perceive as "coming up short" in life is self-inflicted. What we once mistook for being responsible to our future now shows itself to be only an unconscious punishment in the present. Our findings don't mean that we don't take necessary practical actions for our well-being, or that we are not decent to others. It means that we let go of feeling responsible for the future as though we must control its outcome. We realize that there is no way that our painful concern can positively affect any outcome, so we drop that concern. Bit by bit, we begin to hear what Real Life has been trying to tell us all along.

Now is all there is.

The future is not ours to control. Our responsibility may include choices about what's to be, but it is not to determine or suffer over what becomes of our choice.

Our responsibility is only to remain aware in the moment and to allow ourselves to be guided by and within that awareness. It's when we leave it at that, that our experiences become transformational. When we assume false responsibility for any moment to come, and then feel worried about events because of this self-imposed concern, we remain self-formational. Meeting life in this way, we are not transformed by events as we should be.

Think back to the example of the injured athlete we looked at earlier. If he had insisted that his life follow the pattern he had set for himself, he would have been shattered by his accident. Suffering, through anger at himself and the universe, would have been his only experience. Instead, he let himself be carried by life. He allowed life to teach him the transformational lesson, and tragedy was turned to triumph.

Turn to the Power that Transforms You

When we lash out at ourselves for our actions or are anxious about them, these negative feelings are the result of an invisible assumption about responsibility. Our increased understanding, however, reveals that it is not necessary to live with or carry these pains at all. Our false natures protest, saying that if it were not for this sense of responsibility, we would not be effective. The truth is, we can learn to drop the false burden of pain and still perform all the actions we need to in our daily lives. In fact, we'll be even more effective. *There is no necessary relationship between responsibility and suffering.* Our belief in the connection is mistaken, based on self-formational logic. "If I don't suffer over my responsibility," we say, "it would mean that I don't care. But I am a good person, and my suffering proves it." We impose pain on ourselves trying to make ourselves believe that because of it we are worthwhile, and that our self-image is real. It's all a lie. Our suffering does *not* make us real, but seeing through suffering as the false anchor that it is also reveals a new reality where being responsible—and real—are one and the same pleasurable state of Self.

To sum it all up, let's just say that being a truly responsible human being has nothing to do with being an aching human being. The negative emotion, not the task, is the only weight we bear. We mistakenly believe that we can affect what's to be by how willing we are to feel bad over the situation as it is. However, determining the outcome of any event, including our own life, is the task of Truth and Reality. No amount of pained thinking or anxious emotion can affect what will be other than to ensure that it won't be as we wish. This means that our task, in any given moment, is to meet life with awakened awareness so that our understanding of each situation reflects Reality and not our imagined self-interests. Then, the choices emerging from this relationship naturally reflect what is genuinely good for us. Our decisions are increasingly effortless because they are made, literally, in the light of a new understanding.

The esteemed author Ralph Waldo Emerson, himself a self-working student of the Higher Life, reports to us about this bright possibility behind an unseen Reality:

> A little consideration of what takes place around us every day would show us that a higher law than that of our will regulates events; that our painful labors are unnecessary and fruitless; that only in our easy, simple, spontaneous action are we strong. . . . Place yourself in the middle of the stream of power and wisdom which animates all whom it floats, and you are without effort impelled to truth, to right, and a perfect contentment.

Beginning to Take Back Your Life

Everything works out as it should when we are responsible for what we are designed to be responsible for—which is simply to discover the Truth about this life and our place and possibilities within it. When we proceed this way, events unfold perfectly and effortlessly, for something higher carries them for us.

So, whatever it is that wants us to worry—be it a job interview or a failing relationship—just let go of that weight within. Let something else carry it. Our belief that we must wrongly carry the weight of our own lives prevents our transformation into a higher and happier level of being. We can learn how to say to Truth, to God, "You handle it. You carry it." Then we do what seems appropriate, taking the best care we can, and let what happens naturally take care of itself. Remember: we are not on earth to make ourselves real. Our real responsibility is to discover that Reality and ourselves are already One.

Special Summary

> Start suspecting that those anxious thoughts and feelings you catch trying to sell you an umbrella are not there to shelter you from some approaching storm . . . but that their sole purpose is to lure you into one.

———— Guy Finley
The Secret Way of Wonder

6

> *The brave man is not he who feels no fear, for that were stupid and irrational, but he whose noble soul subdues its fear and bravely dares that danger his nature shrinks from.*
>
> — Joanna Baille

YOUR INNER VICTORY CONQUERS ALL

As we learn how to take the higher ground inwardly and begin winning that life for which we are created, we are gradually empowered to prevail over any event and challenge that life presents. Often, to our own amazement, we develop a new kind of eagerness to meet old weaknesses because within us is growing a cosmic confidence that cannot be defeated. Our inner victory rewards us with higher resources that help us every moment of the day. Yes, there are still battles to go through, but the end of the war is in sight: with every passing day the power of the intimate enemy is lessened by our growing love for knowing the truth about ourselves. And in spite of what the false self claims, there is no such thing as negative self-knowledge.

That self that fears, for instance, seeing how afraid you are of someone or some situation will always tell you not to look, or if you already have, that that weakness you've just seen in yourself is bad, something to be ashamed of. Well, *that* self lies. Here's the truth: any part of you that wants you to hide a weakness, or that would hide one from you, is not for you, but is actually against your own best interests.

Here's the proof.

Each time the intimate enemy can convince you to look the other way when sensing something self-defeating going on, it has secretly made you accept that the inner condition you've turned away from is stronger than you. After all, logic reveals that we don't have to hide from what we don't fear. So, if we fear something, it must be greater than us. Do you see the trap here? Agreeing to avoid any inner or outer condition is the same as accepting the false notion that the only alternative is to be defeated by it. This unconscious conclusion serves only one thing: the unconscious fear that wants to keep you serving it. We must get fed up with being afraid of anything, and this new courage comes to us in direct proportion to our willingness to learn the Truth about ourselves. Any one of these truths is more powerful than a million of the lies about our lives that we have all been conditioned, through fear, to live with. Now, here's a great truth to ponder: without the idea of defeat to stand behind it as a consequence of failing to heed that fear, no psychological fear has any power. Take away the whole idea of being defeated in life and fear falls flat on its face. As Guy reveals in his book *Freedom from the Ties that Bind,* the truth is that defeat doesn't really exist:

> *Never Accept Defeat.* As long as it's possible to learn, you need never feel tied down by any past defeat in your life. Here's the real fact: nothing can prevent the inwardly self educating man or woman from succeeding in life. And here's why: *wisdom always triumphs over adversity.* But to win real wisdom calls you to join in a special kind of struggle. And if this battle had a banner under which to rally, here's what would be written upon that higher call to arms: "But I can find out!" Yes, you *can* learn the facts. You may not know the real reasons why you feel so lonely or worried at times, *but you can find out.* And you may not understand how you could have been so blind to that evil person's real intentions, *but you can find out.* Take these four words that are freedom's battle cry. Use them to defeat what's defeating you.

All of these bright facts bring us to a very important stage of our studies together: if it is possible to learn, to grow beyond all past and future self-created grief, what is it within us that doesn't want to see the end of our defeat?

New Self-Knowledge and the Next Step

It's obvious that each of us grows physically without any real inner struggle on our part. Our bodies mature; we learn to tie our shoes, and dance, and do gymnastics. Social skills develop naturally. We grow in our mental abilities as well; we learn a new language, expand our knowledge to grasp a scientific theory, or learn a set of mathematical axioms. This, too, is natural.

However, inwardly, emotionally for instance, while we may develop better ways of covering up the turmoil in our hearts and minds, we never quite outgrow these same old fears and angers, the same doubts and worries. And there is a reason why we don't.

Unlike our physical self which, being under the mechanical laws of evolution, realizes its eventual maturity virtually without any effort, the development of our spiritual self is not evolutionary. It is *voluntary*. Make no mistake. It requires a conscious choice and effort on our part. Genuine inner growth is the pearl of great price, the journey of a thousand steps, the quest of a lifetime. Every one of us is given the opportunity to embark on this great adventure within, but first we must recognize the necessity of it for a complete and fulfilling life. We must fervently desire it. Then we must be willing to go through the necessary self-shocks that this special kind of growth requires. But you won't be alone in this new struggle with yourself as you have been in your old ones. Instead of secret conspirators like the tricky TPICs, you'll have as many strong allies as you're willing to embrace what is true.

Our new self-knowledge enables us to win in life in a new way by revealing that the only time any event can defeat us is when we get tricked into retreating into old reactions and beliefs; when instead of facing the necessary life lessons, we run away by explaining our conflict to ourselves in terms of our old knowledge. As a result, we fail to acquire the true facts that alone lead to our self liberation. We need no longer experience this kind of defeat at our own hands. A way out does exist, but it begins with developing this new approach to life based in higher self-knowledge.

Live in Harmony with Reality

How do we normally develop a new skill? For example, how do we learn to high jump? We listen to instruction, and perhaps we watch someone else; but for the most part, we learn by doing, by trying it ourselves. Generally, with our first attempts we end up crashing into rather than clearing the bar, and when we do, there's no denying it. We can see, and feel, that we've come up short. Our collapsed condition tells us, unmistakably, that we've done something wrong. So now, we try a new angle of approaching the bar, or a new technique of leaving the ground. We do this over and over. And each time we fail to hit the mark, we see we've made a mistake and we alter our behavior, knowing that eventually our self-correction will lift us to the success we desire.

These elementary but exact laws of learning are the same when it comes to our psychological and spiritual development, to winning the war within ourselves. Each time we feel an emotional pain, we should use that as a signal that we've made a mistake, that we've crashed and now need to find and try another new way. For example, our presently pained position is the proof that our past responses to personal crises are inadequate to clear the barriers we still are crashing into—that we not only need a new way to meet life, but that our old ways just don't work. The problem for most of us is that we rarely allow

ourselves to learn in this way. We have hundreds of experiences each day in which our expectations crash into
reality. Whenever this happens, we have what Guy calls a
"close encounter of the truthful kind," because in that
same moment of trial we see for an instant that we really
don't know what to do. These small and large self-crashes
in themselves are not a problem. They are, in a way, the
school of life. The problem is that we won't admit we
don't know what to do. We don't use the event to learn a
new response. Instead, we become defensive and return
to the same mindset that led to our latest collision. We
tell ourselves we understand the cause of getting hurt,
and that we know what or whom to blame. Once we've
assessed fault through this unseen faulty approach, then
we know what to do. Some TPIC pops up and tells us to
"act happy," "eat something," "call a friend," "think about
it." But none of these responses has ever made us better
equipped to handle the next crisis. We persist in our
belief that we know what to do, and instead of trying
something different, we just return to the familiar route.

Remember our example of the high jumper? Imagine
for a moment if every time she crashes she blames the bar
for being in the wrong place! She would never learn the
real nature of her inability to succeed. In the same way,
until we understand where the true cause of our unhappiness lies, we can never be happy. As long as our pre-
conceived notions about life run into the reality of it we
will continue to feel like we're on the losing side, and
since we do not learn from the crash, the process continues. We feel that our lives are out of control, and they are.

We start learning from life when we stop blaming reality, and accept that it was our lack of understanding that created the perceived problem. Our sincere wish to learn cannot fail to attract the healing truth we desire, which can then become a part of us and act through us. This can only happen through our own self-work. No one can tell us the truth, for then it would not become a part of our own nature. Just as the high jumper must try new techniques for herself before she can learn the correct way, we must test our beliefs and question our responses for ourselves. When we begin to understand the truth about reality, and our own place in it (because we have actually entered into it for ourselves), that truth, along with all its power, becomes our own.

The Little Boy Who Laughed Away the "Haunted" House

Reality is very different from our distorted ideas about it, but only our personal experience of this fact can lead to a new way of meeting the events of each day. Unfortunately, we do everything we can to avoid having this kind of experience. There are many parts of us that are secretly afraid that should we earnestly reexamine our ideas about life we'd just stir up some things better left alone. Although if we don't stir them up, we'll never find out that all those things we're afraid of are nothing more than ghosts created by our own minds. Guy illustrated this lesson for us in one of our discussion meetings through the eerie story of four young boys and their encounter with a haunted house.

It all happened in a quiet west Texas town called Turn-around during the years of the Great Depression. This little town really seemed quite ordinary, except for one thing. Right in the heart of it, on one of the main streets leading in and out, stood an old haunted house.

Like most of the people who lived there, our four young boys did everything they could to avoid passing the place. It was rumored that anyone foolhardy enough to venture too close to the creaky old mansion ran the risk of being dragged into its depths by a ghoulish phantom! The boys had no wish for that kind of an adventure, so they went considerably out of their way each morning to reach one of the other streets that would take them to school. It was inconvenient, but there was no help for it. No one in his right mind would pass by the menacing house! So, because every morning the boys took a circuitous route to school, they were usually late getting there. Here, Guy drew a psychological parallel.

We all have things inside of us that we fear: haunting thoughts and dark feelings we sense are down there, but that we'd rather not face for fear they may drag us down into their domain. So instead of questioning any of them, we let them work in the dark while we go out of our way to avoid becoming aware of them. And so it goes. Our lives are unconsciously directed by the invisible hosts dwelling in our internal haunted house. Who are these unseen goblins whose presence we know but upon whose faces we won't look? Think about it for yourself! Isn't anger a demon? Our discomfort at being alone a gloomy specter? And what about that phantom fear of growing old? Instead of looking at these internal chain-rattling entities to see whether or not they *really* have any power to hurt us, we keep them out of sight. Like the children in the town of Turnaround, we walk the other way whenever we distract ourselves from some unwanted condition or blame some outside cause for the way we feel.

There's more. Hidden down there in the same uninvestigated depths of ourselves are beliefs that we hesitate to examine: our theories about God and Reality, about what our true place is in the universe. Most of us have few ideas of our own, relying mostly on what we've taken from others, from books we've read, or things we've heard from seemingly knowledgeable people. So, we're reluctant to examine the validity of these ideas, thinking that if they were proven wrong it would be the same as finding ourselves wrong, and then we'd lose the foundation of our lives. It's one of truth's greatest paradoxes, but exactly the opposite of our entrenched fear holds true: admitting we don't know these things from ourselves is the first step toward Real Knowing and a real life. The extraordinary thing is that, to our present nature, it all seems easier to just ignore these inner issues. Here again, just the opposite holds true: it's the tip-toeing around our own uncertainty and self-confusion that makes our lives so very complicated, and often incomprehensible. Yet, something within us prefers the resulting difficulty to facing what we fear.

Now, the young boys in our story also preferred to go the long way rather than challenge what they believed to be the perils of the haunted house. That is, all the boys except for one. His name was Justin, and he got tired of always going the long way around, of always being late. Then one afternoon on the way home from school, just as they were all about to take their usual detour, Justin turned to his friends and asked, "How do you know it's haunted?"

With the exception of old stories and excitable hearsay, not one of his buddies had a real answer to his question. It was clear. None of the boys knew from firsthand experience what was true of the run-down house and what wasn't. And *this* discovery made something else clear to Justin: he now wanted to know, once and for all, the truth of the matter!

It took some doing, but he convinced his schoolmates to approach the haunted house with him. Sure enough, as they had all predicted, as they drew closer they started hearing strange noises. And just as we always interpret things in a way that proves we're right, the small band of frightened friends took these noises as proof that the house really was haunted, which sent them running away in terror.

But Justin stood steadfast.

"Nobody knows for sure," he told himself over and over again. With his new uncertainty as his only comfort, he ventured up the weed-caked walk toward the already agape front door.

Before he knew it, Justin had stepped inside. At first, the dim light, along with the tension of his drumming heart, caused him to jump at every strange noise. But as he bravely approached and saw through the source of each one, he soon began to laugh in amusement. There was nothing spooky in here. It was just an old house, that's all. Each howl was only the wind passing through age-separated side boards. The rattling sounds that had always made him picture skeletons performing a macabre dance was nothing more than the shaking of some loose window shutters. It really was pretty funny to think that almost the whole town of Turnaround could have been so frightened of a pile of splintering floor boards!

Justin ran out into the light to tell his friends that there was nothing to be afraid of, but not one of them went in to see for himself. Each had his reason: it was late; tomorrow would be better; so on and so on. One boy even said he knew the house wasn't haunted all along. Sure enough, the next day, none of Justin's friends wanted to appear to be a coward, so they all walked with him past the old house on the way to school. But they never stopped looking over their shoulders, and they still jumped at each strange noise until the old house was out of sight. You see, they were secretly still afraid because they had never found out the truth for themselves, but the brave boy who had actually gone inside and investigated the house never jumped. He knew there was nothing in there with any power to hurt him.

It is the same with us. As long as we accept ideas about ourselves and our lives from others, and do not do the work of investigating for ourselves, even our comforting ideas will not be a real help in a crisis. We will always be afraid that something incomprehensible and all-powerful is lurking below the surface. Only the truths that we know from ourselves can sustain us through any storm. We are defeated because we are acting on the basis of artificial truth—false ideas that we never examine and that rarely change based on the lessons of experience. When we discover the Truth for ourselves and let it teach us how to react correctly, we will, as Ralph Waldo Emerson points out, always be victorious:

> So, in regard to disagreeable and formidable things, prudence does not consist in evasion or flight, but in courage. He who wishes to walk in the most peaceful parts of life with any serenity must screw himself up to resolution. Let him front the object of his worst apprehension, and his stoutness will commonly make his fear groundless.

The Right Choice that Keeps You Safe

As events occur, we always assume that we know what they mean for us, and we immediately fall into what feels like the appropriate emotional reaction. That reaction further influences the way we view the following events, and in this way our initial response is "confirmed." An emotional spiral develops that may be very painful, but at the same time can be very exciting, because it gives us a strong sense of who we are. We can now affirm that we are someone who has been mistreated, or tricked, or ignored. We rarely question either our view of events or our response to them. In fact, if someone were to tell us that things were not as we took them to be, we would probably take *that* person as an enemy who cared nothing for us and who was, himself, a part of the threatening situation.

Because we so readily accept the TPIC's interpretation of events as being correct, we rarely investigate to see if another view is possible. As a result, we do not see, for ourselves, that the goblins we fear in our inner "haunted house" are not real at all, and therefore our anxieties continue. Strangely, we prefer to remain ignorant of this error, even though it causes us discomfort. You see, if we realized that we often have a mistaken view of events, it would call into question all the ideas we believe to be true about ourselves and life. It seems less unsettling to simply follow wherever the TPIC of the moment takes us. As we continue to be carried unconsciously from one automatic reaction to another, these conditioned responses grow more entrenched. With repetition, they come to feel more and more natural to us, and the likelihood that we will ever question them continues to diminish. Our behavior grows more deeply settled into these mechanical responses and the way we view events becomes increasingly rigid. As a result, we are taken further away from the spontaneous lives we were meant to enjoy.

As long as we fail to investigate our belief that every strange noise that emerges from the haunted house is what we interpret it to be, we cannot evolve. However, if we will courageously examine every frightening specter to see if it is based in reality, we will eventually discover that there were never any thoughts or emotions that we had to fear. By striving to see ourselves objectively, we learn that all those beliefs about ourselves are not who we really are at all. All of them can be dropped.

Is it possible to understand ourselves so objectively? Can we really become conscious of and question every thought and feeling that tries to take us over? One wintry day as a group of us lingered over lunch, Guy told an encouraging story that addressed this very issue, explaining that while we may fail many times, all our efforts will eventually pay off.

It was the tale of a young prince who, having reached the age of majority, left home to live on a grand estate given to him by his father. He was told that if he ever needed help he was to put a light in the uppermost tower window, and his father would send a special horse and carriage to carry him to safety. However, his father also warned him that an evil wizard, an enemy of the kingdom, lived not too far from his new home. The prince was told to be wary when setting his signal, for this wizard would also see this light and might himself send his own horse and carriage—one that would carry him to danger. Of course, this frightened the young ruler-to-be. After all, how would he be able to tell the difference? His father assured him there was a foolproof measure. Each time, *before* entering the rescue carriage, he was to closely examine the horse pulling it. A light-colored horse would always take him to safety, but a dark horse would always take him to danger.

As the story progressed, many rigors of the ruling life befell the prince, each one causing him to put a light in the window. For many months, because he was too taken over with trying to escape his castle when he felt in danger, he failed to heed his father's warning and neglected to examine the horse that came to get him. As a result he often found himself on one sometimes painful wild ride after another, but before too long the prince realized it was his own inattentiveness that caused him so much distress. Eventually, he found the presence of mind to come awake before entering the carriage each time so that he would remember to examine the horse and determine whether it had been sent by the evil wizard or his father. His growing ability to recognize and refuse the dark horse kept him safe.

This little truth tale is deceptively simple, but before you discount its power to help you defeat the intimate enemy, please consider that the only responses to life's challenges that any of us ride are those we think can carry us to safety. Leaping onto the back of these reactions, according to our old habits, is like entering a runaway carriage being pulled along by runaway thoughts and pounding feelings. Fortunately, like the prince, we can learn to shed the light of reality upon these responses *before* we look to them to carry us to a safe place. Let's look more closely at this life-healing possibility for higher self-protection.

Rise Above All Runaway Reactions

It is not necessary to continue being defeated by our own mechanical responses. We can learn to recognize a dark-horse reaction before we are carried away by it. We already know what many of these runaway reactions are, and so the battle is half won. Fear is dark. Anger is dark. So are anxiety, dread, self-pity, and feeling the whole weight of the world upon our shoulders. Add to this list the dark horses of hatred, revenge, insistence on being right, impatience, and depression—and you have most of those negative states which, if not outright trampling us under their heartless hooves, are certainly sources of unconscious torment.

So you see, knowing the difference between a horse sent by the evil wizard and a horse sent by the good king is not that complicated. It is as simple as recognizing that the wrong horse hurts because its real purpose is to take you on a punishing, pounding ride. You can be sure you've taken the wrong horse and carriage whenever your inner state has you feeling:

- like you've lost control
- frightened by what you see
- angry with yourself or another
- confused or anxious about where you're headed
- pained in your present position
- hatred or resentment for someone else
- sorry you were ever born
- envious of anyone
- desperate for a solution
- certain nothing else counts besides fixing how *you* feel

Now, the truly amazing thing is that in spite of these "rides" that wreck everything from our health to our relationships, we *still* take them! Surely, if we were aware of what we were doing, nothing on earth could convince us to hop on what is hurting us. So, let's see what's happening to cause us to continue making the painful mistake.

An event occurs. We're not sure how to react so we naturally look for help. This is the part of the story where we put a light in the window. We know that a right response is the same as a rescue. And it is. But before we know it, up pops a TPIC. This self always comes complete with the appropriate thoughts and feelings to support why we should let it be in charge of the moment. Simply put, *this* is the dark horse and carriage, and it's there to carry us off. In the past we've always been so grateful for the arrival of that response that told us who we were and what to do that we never questioned it. But now we want to be self-ruling rather than going off on one ride after another to nowhere. We remember the warning the king gave to his son. We know that before we release ourselves into the hands of any automatically appearing rescuing agent we must first take it into the light in order to see who sent it. This royal power to discern dark horses from right ones is already yours, but to wield it, there is a key, a secret step that must be taken. This higher power to choose what will carry us and what won't is only as powerful as our willingness to come to a special kind of psychic pause, an inner halt. Momentarily anchoring ourselves in the fully present moment, we bring our own thoughts and feelings into the light of consciousness to see them for what they are. Once again, that test is fairly clean and simple. In that moment, it's not so much going with what "feels right" as it is basing your choice in seeing what is truly for you; it's knowing without thinking about it that no negative state wants what is right for you.

This exercise of taking a psychic pause may sound as though it would be easy, but it takes practice and persistent effort. You see, it's very tempting to just let ourselves be carried away. In fact, there's nothing to it! Then the rest of our time is spent trying to straighten out the bad rides we've taken. All this not only steals our energy, but also keeps us from being someplace *real*. So now, we're going to take that pause before we believe that any automatic response is the right one. We're going to learn to stay awake. And this awake state is crucial, because the evil wizard is clever. He has tricks that can take a dark horse and make it look bright. For instance, haven't we all had bad spills born out of our own false sense of elation or over-confidence? And a feeling of triumph over the defeat of others can be just as punishing as a state of desolation or anger. With time, we learn to take no horse at face value. When in doubt, try to recall this axiom: The proof of the horse is in the ride. If the ride is punishing or meandering, we're in the wrong carriage.

Now, suppose we wake up and realize our position too late, *after* we've entered the wrong carriage and are already rolling along. Perhaps we see that we're being dragged along by a state of anxiety or anger In the past we always accepted these negativities as being appropriate reactions, but now we recognize them as being wrong for us and unnecessary. We no longer want their direction to be our own. What do we do now?

First, we shouldn't try to stop the horse. It's a waste of energy. So is trying to convince ourselves that we're not in that state, or feeling guilty about it, or fighting it in any other way. These choices are just back-up dark horses! The only way out is for you to choose to just come wide awake. This conscious choice transforms us from a person who is completely identified with the runaway state into a person who is aware of it. Through that awareness we jump out of the wild carriage back into the safety, sanity, and solid ground of the present moment.

Jumping clear of your own jumbled selves takes special skills, but these come to you as you see the need for them. So, don't get discouraged. Stay off of that horse! You may fail many times before you jump clear successfully, but look at the progress we've made already. We now know that we tend to get on wrong carriages, and that it's not necessary to do so—those thoughts and feelings are not who we really are. Our aim is now to try to be aware and know what's happening, so we don't fall into the same mistake again and again. When we see ourselves looking for a reaction and putting a light in the window, we know there's a strong possibility that the wrong horse is likely to arrive. Therefore, we make an effort to determine the quality of the "help" that comes to get us by first choosing to help ourselves by stepping back from our own rush to be rescued. Standing apart in this way is the only way to see whether the arriving solution is, for us in that moment, true or false.

On a deeper level, this new understanding of ours and the choices it allows leads us to an even bigger step toward winning the inner war. We have come to realize that we live in an internal country where there are, indeed, forces set up against us. Our growing awareness of this intimate enemy and the way it tricks us into a self-harming reaction brings us closer to victory.

Let Truth Help You Win Yourself

The story about Justin, the young boy who grew tired of being afraid, and the story of the young prince who learned not to get into the wrong carriage reveal the same powerful lesson. They teach us that we must begin to investigate our own thoughts and feelings to see that what we have always accepted as necessary and natural reactions are often nothing more than automatic impositions of the false self. Our gradually increasing self-knowledge empowers us to see through these unconscious responses which, at the same time, shows us the secret of being a truly self-ruling individual.

Even though it is our birthright to be self-determining, this spiritual power has its price. If we're to reclaim our inner lives from the intimate enemy, we must dare to act upon our new understanding instead of allowing our old nature to decide our course. In short, we must not automatically ride off on our first, usual reaction to any event. Every time we meet a moment where there is a shock, instead of trying to take control of it by turning to a familiar response to rescue us, we must recognize that we don't really know what to do and leave a space for the Truth to show us the reality of the situation. As a simple example, but one that speaks volumes about this lesson, suppose we hear that a friend made an unkind comment about us. If we follow the old reaction that insists we must get negative by that news, we're carried off in an angry or desperate carriage. If we take that psychic pause that empowers, and in it allow Reality to show us that our Real Self cannot be hurt—or betrayed—then we are free!

Don't be afraid to *not* have the familiar response. Let it fall away. Just be empty for the moment of all recognizable reactions, and don't fill this temporary emptiness with old familiar ideas. The TPIC telling you you're in danger is itself responsible for the fear you feel. See through this false self each time, and you'll not only reach the safety you've always longed for, you'll discover that who you really are never had anything to fear.

Have you ever seen pictures of a huge ice breaker forging its way through miles of frozen water, easily cutting through every obstacle in its path? Don't we each long for that kind of strength for ourselves? We all wish to break through inner and outer barriers, to go where we want, when we want, and at our own speed. We want our lives to belong to us. This is what winning the war within ourselves is all about. It's about little by little breaking through the frozen beliefs and feelings that have made an enemy of life through our own distorted interpretations and mechanical reactions.

To make real inner progress, get spiritually reckless. Avoid nothing. Let whatever shaking you must do be your waking! And listen to me: you don't have to be strong; you just have to be tired of trembling before life.

The only way to defeat the intimate enemy is by deliberately stepping into its domain—that "haunted house," whatever its nature—armed only with the light of reality. Since no dark condition can remain in power in the presence of your enlightened understanding of it, victory is yours. Which is the same as saying you have won back your life.

Special Summary

> Most men and women searching for the secret
> of letting go make one mistake in common.
> They listen to their own conclusions. This is
> tragic. In as many ways possible, the Truth
> is trying to teach us that the limit of our
> present life-level is not the limit of life's
> possibilities. . . . What is possible for us to
> become only truly changes when we are
> willing to see what is impossible for us to
> continue being. This is the Secret of Secrets.
> This is the secret of letting go.

—Guy Finley
The Secret of Letting Go

7

> *Order means light and peace, inward liberty and free command over one's self; order is power.*

— Amiel

THE AUTHORITY TO RECLAIM YOUR LIFE

As we have seen, the war within is waged by conflicting parts of our own selves. It is this inner division that is the cause of all the dissension and heartache. We all know what it's like to be caught in this internal struggle, for the mechanical mind creates it in every one of us. As spiritual seekers, this inner battle involves an additional element: the conflict between those few right parts of us that question the necessity of these inner collisions and wish finally to arrive at the peaceful life, and the many wrong parts that prefer to remain on the battlefield. Religious history is filled with accounts of sincere individuals who witnessed this personal struggle. As St. Paul so touchingly put it, "The good I wish to do, I do not do; and instead I do the evil I wish not to do."

Looking closely at ourselves, an honest self-appraisal reveals that no one, strong, authoritative voice is giving us direction. Instead, many disparate voices vie for power. As we now know, the cause of the resulting confusion and unhappiness lies in all those self-centered, touchy TPICs that insist, one after the other, that the world conform to their demands. It's a cacophony of voices inside, each one screaming for attention; each one oblivious to the others and to reality itself; each one insisting that it is who we really are. As we are whipsawed from one self to another, the decisions of one may no longer be matched by the desires of another. Something in us watches it all in despair, knowing there is nothing in control. We vow to work harder so that one day we can fulfill our goal of becoming a person with a steady, complete nature. But then, before we know it, we're caught up in yet another battle for some illusive prize and forget all our good intentions.

Is there any way to get off the battlefield altogether and win back our lives?

Is it possible for the right parts within us to prevail? Can one strong, right voice overwhelm all the others?

Yes! It *is* possible to find that right authority within. The transformation occurs naturally when we first see our situation fully, and then wish to remove ourselves from it above all else. As that right intention grows in strength, a magic method can be shown to us that will actually take us off the battlefield psychologically, even while we stay right where we are!

The War Correspondent's Amazing Discovery

One Wednesday evening at class, Guy spoke to us about self-transformation. That night he told us an especially powerful story that took us to a faraway place and introduced us to a young war correspondent.

As the story unfolded, we found ourselves traveling back to the 1960s, where we met a young reporter who had volunteered to go to Vietnam to interview the men and women on duty there. His assignment was to record their experiences so that his readers back home would have a better understanding of the events of the war. On his arrival in the war-torn country, he found himself immersed in a truly fiendish place. The most disturbing element of all was the difficulty in recognizing friends from enemies. It soon became clear that no one was to be trusted.

One evening as the young reporter dined at a local restaurant, he caught wind of some hastily whispered rumors about unusual activity developing in the jungles to the north. Thinking that this might be the opportunity he had been waiting for, he gathered his gear and headed off for what he hoped would be his Pulitzer Prize-winning story. For a moment, as he became aware of these thoughts, he was heartsick to see how his own ambition and selfishness sought to turn a tragic event for others to his own glory. This self-revelation disturbed him, but pushing it away, he jumped on the transporter that was about to take him to a very different story than the one he was expecting to find.

Upon reaching his destination, the journalist was greeted by a young man who called out, "Welcome to Camp Crazy." That night the place proved true to its name. As soon as darkness fell, the sky lit up with rockets and mortar fire. With each deafening blast, the very earth seemed to shake. The terrified reporter ran to a huge underground bunker where hundreds of men were settling in for the long night ahead. Taking in the confusion of men, the noise, and the flickering lights, he knew he was in a kind of hell. "What am I doing here?" he asked himself. The only answer he received was another booming explosion that caused the lamps to swing dizzily from the makeshift ceiling. In spite of his nervousness, his instincts as a reporter were still active, and he listened intently to the snatches of conversation around him. What he heard only added to his shock. In one corner a group of soldiers were plotting against their officers. At a table to the left the men were arguing among themselves, and it appeared that a fist fight was imminent. Fear and violence filled the room.

As he continued to look around, however, something different began to nag at the reporter. He began to sense that something was out of place within all this madness. Passing his eyes back and forth across the room, he finally saw what it was. In the far corner a man was sitting calmly, completely detached from the disorder around him. Appearing not to have a care in the world, it was as though he were sitting in the eye of the whirling storm. The reporter watched the fellow more carefully to see if perhaps he was drugged, but the alert expression on his face made it clear he was not. The reporter wondered if perhaps he had now found a real story within the madness of Camp Crazy.

Walking over to the serene soldier, the young journalist was met by a genuine smile. After a few opening comments the correspondent could no longer contain his curiosity. "What's going on here?" he asked. "How is it that everyone else is anxious and hateful, but you seem calm, and even happy?"

The soldier looked at him and laughed knowingly. "It's no secret," he explained. "It's just that some weeks ago I put in for a transfer, and I just got word that I'm being sent back home in the morning."

Now the reporter understood why the man was in a different state from all the others. He wasn't part of this world anymore, so it didn't frighten him. He was no longer involved. He had put in for a transfer.

Transfer Yourself into a New Life

The spiritual life is all about discovering the need for, and putting in for a transfer. It's about seeing that our present psychological world is really just a secret battlefield that makes no sense. We try to make sense of the war within by taking sides in it. The only thing this accomplishes is to get us further embroiled in the battle, for example, when a value we've acquired (perhaps becoming a success) comes into conflict with a desire striving for fulfillment (the wish just to have fun). The ambitious part criticizes and tries to control the lazy part, resulting in a person who resents working, but feels guilty when play-ing. Every self-criticism is equivalent to a rocket attack. Every self-pitying thought is a blast of mortar fire. As these TPICs displace one another at dizzying speed, we find ourselves being unhappy whatever we do. We hope that by taking the right side, we will eventually find someplace where there's peace, but no matter where we look, we still find ourselves in a battle with ourselves about ourselves, being buffeted about by unconscious opposites. There seems no escape from this inner condi-tion until we begin to see it for what it really is. Then vic-tory becomes possible. To paraphrase the words of Hui-Hai, freedom finally comes to that mind which *has reached the state in which the opposites are seen as empty.* In other words, in the context of this study, it is just one TPIC, one self-image, fighting with another. There is only one way to get out, and that is to see the truth of these facts, which is the same as putting in for a transfer.

As Guy explains, we're supposed to live in a constant state of transfer. This idea can be said in another way by paraphrasing Christ: we are meant to be in this world, but not of it. However, instead of enjoying this transcen-dent life, we inhabit a warring world within us created by our own thoughts, and then we suffer the constant attacks and counterattacks that are the unhappy natural result. It is not necessary to continue in this way. When we can see an attack coming, we have the ability to put in for a transfer. This special kind of spiritual transfer hap-pens when we turn our attention away from the battling thoughts, step off the battlefield, and turn the whole thing over to something Higher. We know that there is no possibility for anything but more fighting as long as we focus on the screaming thoughts and our attempts to pacify them. How can we achieve a cease fire between the warring parties when we ourselves are secretly both sides of the conflict? When an attack is launched and we feel the blast, we always look for some corner of safety in the world of our own thoughts, but it will never be found there. We'll only find safety by realizing that the world of battles is nonsensical, and then put in for a transfer. At the moment we see the futility of all our attempts and step off the battlefield altogether, that action allows the entrance of something True into our lives that is, and always has been, above the battle.

Leave Your Troubles Behind You Where They Belong

We will take the first right steps toward putting in for a transfer when we reach the point of wanting a life of inner peace more than anything else. We know we have not achieved that free life when we find ourselves trapped in the bunker, enduring the fighting within and fearfully awaiting the next bomb blast. Why don't we act in our own best interests when we see how we've been hurting ourselves? Why don't we make our escape? We each hold many wrong attitudes that keep us from putting in for a transfer at that point. For one thing, we still hope to gain some kind of advantage from it all, like the reporter's wish to be awarded the Pulitzer Prize. Then, we continue to believe that there is a possibility of winning the war. And if not, at least there is that strange sense of satisfaction we experience when the fire and shelling, and our hatred of it, provides us with a strong sense of ourselves—fiery feelings that we call "being alive." Temporarily filled by these powerful emotional states, there are parts of us that actually enjoy the fury of the battle. It fills us with excitement and a sense of importance. But there's another even more deeply hidden reason why we don't ask for a transfer: we're secretly afraid that there may not be any place to transfer to.

This is why it is so important to discover, through self-observation, the truth about our minute-to-minute battles. When we become fully aware of just how dark these warring worlds within us really are, we no longer wish to remain there, no matter what the cost. Happily, our efforts to escape *must* meet with success. Here's why: that hostile world we wish to leave is no more than the artificial world of our own false self, and any time we can wake up from its view of life, it's the same as winning, in that moment, a transfer into a new world where war just doesn't exist. Waking up and the way out are one and the same act: leaping into full consciousness in the present moment. In this place there is no "war," no "me" in danger, but only the safety and quiet of reality. By turning our attention away from the battles within, we can begin to hear the higher guiding voice that has nothing to do with the madness inside. Within the present moment is all the help we need.

We must make a sincere effort to request a transfer all the time, but how can we accomplish this when everything within and outside of us tries to keep us as we are? The good news is that if we'll only struggle to stay awake to ourselves, the reminders are all around us. Every time we feel a pain, we can remember that the reason why we suffer that pain is because some TPIC has wandered onto a battlefield of its own making. We believed we were compelled to stay on that battlefield and fight. Now we know that we don't have to remain identified with this false self that feels itself to be under attack. This is what wishing for a transfer means—that we no longer wish to be *that* false self—or any other. We want no more of this endless thinking and feeling that bring us no place but back to our old sad selves. We've had more than enough of the shelling and sneak attacks. We want to transfer out.

Be assured that the more we see we are embroiled in battles that can't be won, the more we wish to be transferred out. As this wish grows stronger and more pervasive, it brings us back to Reality more frequently. Not only do we remember to wish for a transfer when we're in pain, but even during those times when we experience pleasure, we remain aware that the source of all goodness is above the battlefield, and *that* is where we want to be. No matter where we are, or what we are doing, we desire the permanent goodness of life outside of the war zone, and that helps us remember that our primary aim is to achieve a transfer.

To start becoming aware that the world created by a confused human mind isn't the true world, even while we continue to pursue our daily lives, is to begin to be conscious of another higher world, that is our true home. We are here to learn the lessons of this life, not to be drawn unconsciously into its battles. We each have the opportunity to make that crucial connection to something real that lies above all battlefields. We reach for that opportunity each time our own awakened awareness requests, "Please transfer me." If, after we have made the request, the transfer does not come, we must examine ourselves to see the many false parts of us that do not want to leave. No matter. A right wish must eventually win out. We need simply start all over and make the request again. We may grow impatient waiting, but we will never be hurt on the battlefield as long as we remember that our one aim is to leave it.

Why Asking for a Higher View Makes a Happier You

Putting in for a transfer doesn't mean that we physically leave or otherwise avoid the naturally occurring challenges of this world. To the contrary, the opening lines of one of my favorite poems by Guy exhorts its reader:

> Let us fall in battle
> And not upon the run.
> The enemy is before us,
> We know what must be done.

To put in for a transfer from our troubles means that we learn to use them rather than being used up by them. We discover how to rise above our own present psychology. In this way we continue to encounter life's many events and challenges, but we are no longer affected by them negatively as we once were because we no longer see them the same way. Guy told us another one of his marvelous stories to illustrate this point; it was a fanciful tale about "Michael the Mighty Ram."

Michael the Mighty Ram was one of a flock of sheep and ewes that lived on a very inhospitable mountainside. Most of the flock were miserable, and if you looked at the facts of their daily existence, there appeared to be good reason for it. Every day, late in the afternoon, swarms of stinging flies came out that tormented the sheep and caused them, in their agony, to turn on one another. Then, early each morning, the sheep were nervously aroused from a fitful sleep by their fear of the prowling cougars that stalked them at daybreak. Again, in their fear, they would turn on one another. Pushing and shoving in a desperate attempt to find a safe place to stand, they only added to one another's pain.

In many ways, those sheep are very much like unhappy human beings. We also suffer from things that seem to be outside of our control; and in our attempts to ease our own pain we either attack others, or turn inward and become self-enclosed. We focus our attention on the difficulty and the discomfort it brings. Soon, we can't see anything except for the one problem that seems to engulf us, and in our desperation we are not capable of looking beyond that problem to find a solution. We accept the problem on its own terms, as a necessity, and fail to see that we have the power to remove ourselves completely from that problem's sphere any time we wish. It's not negative to become aware of how our limited thinking causes us to perpetuate our unhappiness. It is negative to continue to find reasons to be unhappy. Don't we all know men and women who are very much like these bickering, petty ewes and rams? They fall helpless before every perceived difficulty, and then direct their bad humor against everyone else.

Now within this flock of sheep, one young ram and one young ewe began to question whether it was necessary to live in this uncomfortable way. They didn't want to have to put up with it anymore, and they wondered if perhaps there were another kind of life possible for them. The young ram and ewe had many soul-searching discussions with one another over the matter, and they also applied themselves to examining the behavior of the other sheep in an effort to understand better what was happening to them.

One day their investigations led them to a remarkable discovery. They noticed one old ram, we'll call him Michael, who never fought with anyone. Unlike the other sheep who were always worried about one thing or another, he seemed always to be untroubled. They never saw him in an irritable state. His life was clearly not in the same rut as all the others!

Feeling certain that Michael the Mighty Ram would be able to impart some great wisdom to them, the young ram and ewe approached him and asked if he would tell them his secret. Michael nodded his great horned head in approval. In all the years he had been with the group, these two were the first to ever ask him such a question. He commented that the other sheep in the flock just suffered unconsciously, and that this form of unconscious suffering is endless. He went on to tell them that the only way to finally be relieved of the torment and begin enjoying a free life is to question the necessity of any negative condition. With this, Michael then promised that he would reveal to them the next day the reason why he was not bothered by the things that drove the other sheep to distraction.

The young ram and ewe could hardly wait for the next day to break, and sure enough, Michael the Mighty Ram was true to his word. Around 4 o'clock the following afternoon, when the stinging flies started to gather, he led them through a hidden crevice in the mountainside and onto a ledge that, until that moment, they never knew existed. There he showed them how to slip into a space between two vertical cliffs that formed a natural wind tunnel. Because of the wind, the insects avoided the area altogether. Enjoying the sweet grass and the warm afternoon sun, the happy trio spent the day undisturbed. At 6:30, by natural law, the flies departed, and Michael led out the young ram and ewe.

The next morning Michael taught them another valuable lesson. It was time for the cougars to prowl, and the flock of sheep was restless and afraid. But the young ram and ewe saw that Michael was standing on the high ground where he had a commanding view of the entire area. Nothing could ever sneak up on him. Putting together their observations about the flies and the cougars, the young ram and ewe fully understood Michael's secret. There was never any need to suffer. It was just a matter of positioning. The place where a ram positioned himself had everything to do with his quality of life.

Put Yourself Where Freedom Finds You

An inner place of safety exists. If we stand in that new position, no dark feelings can affect us. That position has always been there, waiting for us to find it. It is the place where the True Self resides. But we have mistakenly believed that only two options were open to us: to either stand and suffer, or run away and suffer, with our problems in constant pursuit. We always listened to the inner flock of sheep that bleated fearfully, "submit to the suffering," "find some way to deal with it," "hate whatever put you in pain."

As long as we continue to respond to the suffering in this way, believing in its inevitability, it is in control. However, a way out does exist. It is to stop thinking along those familiar lines so that a right spirit can come in and guide us to a new internal position. We begin by realizing, little by little, that our current position is intolerable. When we get tired of putting up with those intolerable conditions, we begin to look around for another answer. Then we can be led to a new position where we are safe from the stinging flies and stalking cougars of our own negative thoughts. When we stand between the soaring cliffs of self-knowledge and the desire to live above the pettiness of this world, the dark thoughts lose their power to touch us.

A critical step in bringing about this transfer to a new position is to develop a clear purpose for ourselves, for our position in life is very much intertwined with what we believe to be our purpose in life. When, like the foolish sheep, our only purpose is to eat, mingle, mate, or rule the herd, we position ourselves accordingly, and end up right in the middle of the battlefield. That foolish purpose invites the attacks that cause our suffering, and allows them to continue. When our new purpose is to live the higher life we were meant to enjoy, our attention rises above the frightened flock to the cliffs and the sky above. Our search in this new place is rewarded. A new, safe position is revealed to us. Here we can find a life free from suffering, as well as experience a new energy and purpose in our lives. In the words of Yuan-Wu:

> If you understand, you can make use of it on the road, like a dragon reaching the water, like a tiger in the mountains. If you don't understand, then the worldly truth will prevail, and you will be like a ram caught in a fence, like a fool watching over a stump waiting for a rabbit."

Let's look at what all of this means for us psychologically. What is our daily life really like now? Does the following description seem pretty accurate?

Free Yourself from Every False Authority

Each day we hear a knock on our psychological door, and when we open it a pushy person enters and begins to bark out orders: "Worry about this." "Remember and regret that." "Speed up your driving so that other car can't get ahead of you." "Work, work, work."

Is it little wonder we experience only the most fleeting feelings of love, kindness or relaxation? We're being driven by something that calls itself an authority, and without ever questioning accept it as one. A voice comes in (that is, a TPIC pops up) and orders us to become negative. We obey without even being aware of the voice. We think that we ourselves are responsible for that reaction, and that there's a good reason for it. We've been conditioned to accept these sad, self-destructive states as natural. At the same time, another part of us hates our darkened state and thinks that this hatred is natural. However, a more informed view reveals to us that neither the wrong state, nor the hatred of the state are natural, and we don't have to put up with either any longer. Our new and higher self-understanding makes it possible for us to regain command over our lives, so we need never have to obey those dark inner voices again.

The time has come to take back our lives. If we fail to do so, all we have to look forward to is hearing a new knock on our inner door again and again, and then finding ourselves admitting an unconscious, unhappy force that tells us what to do. Oh, it's true that sometimes the unwelcome visitor brings a cake (a happy thought), and we feel temporarily content. But for every cake a TPIC brings, it whispers ten painful suggestions. We can begin to recognize that all of these inner voices are false author-ities, and instead of inventing ways with which to tolerate them, *we can challenge their right to exist altogether.* It is not possible for two authorities to rule. When we challenge and reveal for ourselves the false authority, we make an opening for the true one to take its rightful place.

Take Back Authority over Your Own Life

We can break the control of these inner voices with their false authority. When we begin to feel the approach of a negative state, we can boldly challenge it by coming wide awake and inwardly asking, "What is your authority based on?" Our ability to consciously question these inner intruders is enhanced as we clarify our purpose in life. Our new and higher purpose to break free leads us always to choose the high ground, and from that higher vantage point, we can see the approach of any negative state before it takes us over. With experience, we become more adept at recognizing the conditions that tend to give rise to these pained TPICs. Because we know they have no real exis-tence in themselves, and will pass if we do not feed them our own energy, freedom is always within our reach.

What a new way to look at life! Until now, no one ever told us that our mental and emotional suffering had no right to have authority over us. In fact, we were told, or shown, just the opposite. Now, with our redefined pur-pose, we no longer see the value in a life that can be disrupted at any moment by a negative state that comes in and tells us how we must feel. We realize it's time to take to the High Ground within.

If a man took the same road every day, and every day he had an accident on that road, wouldn't it make sense for him to start taking a different road? You would expect him to make a connection between the road he was taking and his life of accidents and then to seek out a new road, a new way. In the same way, we must begin to understand that there is an inner connection between the place where we are and the psychological accidents we experience. We must resolve to no longer suffer unconsciously. That means that the next time the flies of dark thoughts attack and the cougars of negative states prowl, instead of dealing with the disturbance on its own terms, we will seek the new and higher position within that is disturbance free. Our purpose in life will be to challenge and rise above every wrong feeling by finding the higher ground within where who we are is out of the reach of any punishing thought.

It is important that we not get discouraged, even if we fail in our new purpose many times. We have all been deeply conditioned to long for and seek out our lives amongst the flock, with all its temporary pleasures and abiding difficulties. That's what we're used to. It's one aspect of our nature, but the mighty nature of Michael is within us as well. A true authority lives inside each of us that would no more submit to a false state than any creature would voluntarily jump off a cliff into a treacherous ravine. We can invoke that true authority by making it our purpose to release its power into our lives. Be assured that everything we do to free ourselves and discover who we really are produces a positive result, which is the same as saying that our sincere attempts to liberate ourselves must succeed!

Each time we choose in favor of our higher purpose, our position is redefined and we are shown life in a new way. Each bit of new knowledge increases our strength to take our lives back. Every day provides another opportunity for us to reach the understanding that just because something is pervasive does not necessarily make it powerful. Now we see that our wrong assumptions and demands kept us in a position where suffering seemed natural. Our new position shows us that none of that was real. We can challenge the authority of the false to take us over. We can say to it, "I don't want to live with you anymore." And, remarkably, everything will change.

The Power of Being Single-Minded

If we are to succeed at taking back authority over our lives, we must persist. After all, as we're learning in this important study, we have many years of wrong thinking and negative emotions to see through. As we become more familiar with the wrong powers that have been ruling our lives all along, we discover many disturbing things within. With these new discoveries, it may even feel sometimes as though we're getting worse, not better.

In fact, everything we see is good for us. We're just beginning to face honestly how bad it has been all along, and
that is the first step to real inner newness.

Many great spiritual teachers warn us not to fall for the
trick of discouragement. We are told to face the rigors of
the inner journey in good spirits. Vernon Howard says we
may have to knock on the door of truth ten thousand
times before it will answer. But *it will answer,* and then all
the effort will be rewarded a thousandfold.

Guy tells us the cautionary tale of a man who hears
that there is gold in the mountains, and goes in pursuit.
Then, finding only three small flakes in what seems to
him to be a very long time, declares that there is no gold
to speak of and stops the search. In contrast to that foolish man, we should be delighted to have acquired those
three flakes, and take that as all the encouragement we
need to redouble our efforts. The reason we get discouraged is because we don't know the value of spiritual gold.
The happy fact is that even one flake, when combined
with another, yields something that is greater than the
sum of the parts. We can take two spiritual facts, put
them together, and come up with a new understanding
that is much more powerful than either fact alone—one
that will speed us along on our journey home.

For example, one day you might read a spiritual para-
ble that explains that for the seed to give rise to a new
plant, it must fall to the ground and die to its old self.
Another day, you may catch one of your false TPICs in

the act of taking over. Your awareness stops it in its tracks. Although you know the rightness of seeing it, you also sense a feeling of loss as a familiar feeling fades away. If at that point you remember the lesson about the seed, you come to a new awareness of the meaning of the death of the false self, and how that death gives rise to the Real You. A powerful understanding is given to you that changes the way you now see everything you do, and everything you ever thought you were. Two simple facts were brought together, and in their combination opened a new world of meaning to you. None of us knows how much spiritual gold we've gathered as a result of our sincere efforts. Nor do we know when those pieces will come together to form a new power. We must patiently continue with our work, secure in the knowledge that the coming of the self-victory we now seek is as much under law as is the certainty of our continued captivity if we remain the same.

There is tremendous power in having a single direction and persisting without wavering. Our enduring, fervent wish to understand higher principles such as those outlined in this chapter invites the revelations that will eventually lead us to our higher, safe position. Our persistent desire for the Truth enables us to ultimately harness the energy of the universe. In that energy lies the authority to take back our lives.

Special Summary

> *From this moment forward, consciously*
> *challenge the right of any dark disturbance*
> *to direct your life. Stand your inner ground*
> *until its demands drain away. Negative states*
> *have no real life of their own, so consciously*
> *withdrawing your life from theirs is the same*
> *as commanding their dark presence to fade.*

—Guy Finley
Freedom from the Ties That Bind

8

> *Who is there who can make muddy*
> *waters clear? But if allowed to remain*
> *still, it will gradually clear itself.*

— Lao-tsu

START ENLARGING YOUR WORLD WITH SELF-STUDY

The waves broke gently on the shore and washed the moonlit beach with silver. The two young couples walked in silence as the water foamed up around their feet and rushed back to the waiting sea—a perfect evening. Suddenly one of the young women pointed up at the brilliant night sky and called out, "Look, a shooting star."

They all turned, but it was too late. Except for the twinkling of the stars, the sky was still once more.

The woman's husband seemed especially agitated. "I don't understand it," he complained. "You have all the luck. I'm always hoping to see a shooting star, but never do. And you always seem to see them. Why is that?"

151

The young woman shrugged her shoulders, and smiled playfully. "I don't know," she said. "Maybe it's because I'm always looking for them."

This short story provides us with a special insight that is simple on the surface, but hides a much deeper lesson. For starters, we can't hope to find what we aren't looking for. Simple enough. Now let's look at the same idea from a slightly different angle, which will increase its depth. What we "find" in life, in other words, what our lives are filled with moment to moment, is always a result of where we have our attention.

For example, going back to our story, where did the three companions of the "lucky" young woman have their attention at the moment of the shooting star?

One of the men was thinking about a business deal he was working on, and was trying to decide whether or not to make a certain phone call when he got back to the city on Monday morning. The second young man was reliving an argument he'd had with his father earlier in the week, growing more annoyed as he remembered how his father seemed unable to appreciate the fact that he was now a grown man with a family of his own. The other young woman, who was soon to move into her new home, had her mind otherwise occupied with rearranging the furniture!

The truth is that each of them was an unsuspecting captive in a small world of his or her own making, so that not one of them knew where he or she was. They did not see the splendor of the starlit sky; they did not feel the power of the boundless ocean as it breathed peacefully, like a great beast at rest; nor were they fully aware of one another. They could not be. For while their bodies may have been walking along the shore that evening, each person's attention was far, far away—in another space and time.

And so it is with most human beings.

Convinced that the limited world their own thoughts reveal is the only world there is—and that this world holds the only possibilities there are—they spend the predominant part of their earthly lives being washed back and forth within the confined space between their past memories and future hopes. The "reality" of this, their tiny thought world, goes on virtually unquestioned because contained within it are loads of secretly self-circling emotions like fear, sadness, anger, and false excitements; strong—but empty—feelings that provide lots of ups and downs, but that actually go nowhere. All that can happen herein is that the spiral of their lives shrinks. The smaller their world becomes, which under law it must, the more unhappy they become. In their unaware state, these men and women do not understand that their sadness and stress belong only to the small world they have mistakenly called their home, and nothing else.

Let's return to our young heroine. How was it that she caught sight of the star as it flashed in that glorious moment? In her heart she had always felt the pull toward a larger world. Sensing that she, herself, was the only one responsible for her being trapped in a prison of thought, she had worked hard on herself for many years, struggling to be free. On that very evening, in fact, several times as they walked along she had been tempted to sink back into herself and focus her attention on her concerns over money, a pair of shoes she wanted to buy, her desire to have a child. But not wanting to be pulled into that small world, she had been watching her thoughts, and managed to catch herself each time before she was completely engulfed. She kept forcing herself back into the awareness of the beach, to the sound of the waves and the cool sand beneath her feet; *back to the present moment*. It was during one of those moments that she looked up and saw her shooting star: a reward from reality itself for working to set her sights above her self.

That shooting star was not her only reward that evening. Not too much later that same night, while lying in bed, there was another flash across her awareness; only this time, it came as a sudden insight into her own True Nature. As she lay there, enjoying the quiet of her own contented breathing, she had the sudden sensing that the selfsame power that moved the endless ocean waves was expressed within her own in-and-out breaths. For a moment, she knew she was not separate from that one supreme energy source, and this great glimpse brought with it a new kind of light that lit up every corner of her innermost being. And when she awakened the next morning she had the feeling her life would never again be the same.

So, our summer story closes. On that warm starlit night four friends had walked down a deserted beach, and for three of them, nothing remarkable happened except their separate worlds drew a little tighter. The fourth took one step further outside of herself toward a life of Reality and freedom. She had fought a short struggle with the intimate enemy and had won for herself the first in a series of truly timeless victories.

There is so much more for each of us to experience than the closed world reported to us by our limited senses and habitual thoughts. Everywhere Reality's messages flash like shooting stars to lead us outside of ourselves and our self-imposed isolation. When a rare individual responds to those messages, and feels their pull, this is the beginning of the wonderful process of inner change and the breaking down of every inner wall. Since you are now reading this book, you have probably felt this pull. You, too, sense that you are not inwardly free, and you want to experience that expansive life you are meant to enjoy.

How do we achieve this life liberation? The lessons and exercises in this book are a secret escape plan. They are a means of freeing ourselves from the intimate enemy. The key to the entire process is contained in self-study.

"Know thyself" is perhaps the oldest, wisest, deepest, and most succinct spiritual instruction ever given. In fact, it is our nature to know ourselves. To one degree or another, each of us is born with the inner longing to seek out and to discover our True Essence. However, almost from the very beginning of our young lives, our efforts are misdirected. Our hopes and aspirations for meaningful answers are placed outside of us. So, instead of pursuing the "pearl of great price" lying within us, we wind up pursuing people, places, and things that we hope will finally be able to reveal to us just who we are. Yet, no acquisition, or any sense of self its pursuit may provide, brings us that permanent sense of self we desire. It cannot, for that outer world, by its very nature, is nothing but continuous change. This is why, if we want to find ourselves, there is no substitute for self-study.

Self-study is what leads to coming to know ourselves as we truly are. It is the only way we become familiar with the thought self and its many fleeting TPICs. And like the young Prince we met in chapter 6 who learned how to avoid getting into the wrong carriage, self-study is how we begin empowering ourselves not to just automatically go where every TPIC would lead us. As a higher benefit, our self-study allows us to hear and heed that still small Voice within us which not only corrects our life course, but connects us to ever higher and happier experiences along the way.

How do we go about doing this true inner work? How do we succeed with our self-study?

How Higher Self-Study Helps Reveal Your Higher Self

Let us start by seeing what self-study is not. Although self-study may include reading certain inner life books or listening to lectures on self-transformation, these materials, as encouraging and informative as they may be, are really only preparational tools; and they have their place. After all, if you were going to climb a mountain, you would want expert advice on the proper equipment to use, and you would want instruction from others who had climbed that mountain before you. From their past painful experiences, you might be able to save a few of your own! Or so the thinking goes. All of this instruction, however, cannot raise you one inch above the valley floor to bring you any closer to the mountain top. There is only one way to reach the peak: you, *yourself,* must make the climb.

In the same way, self-study is personal, individual work that sincere seekers must do for themselves. Far more intricate and at least as rigorous as trying to scale a real mountain, self-study asks us to begin with:

- Honestly observing ourselves as often as possible during the day to see the truth of what is *actually* directing our life in those moments

- Actively meeting each moment of life with a wish to understand our inner condition instead of looking for ways to justify it

- Living from a new center of gravity in ourselves: where our one prevailing wish is to see those Truths about our daily experiences that might serve to change us, instead of trying to explain away our experiences in an effort to protect what we hope is true

- Taking small but definite steps into some personally challenging condition instead of mechanically avoiding it—just to see if any psychological fear ever tells you the truth

- Being willing to step outside some TPIC's point of view to see that it may be more short-sighted than first glance reported

- Suspending negative emotional reactions long enough to learn something about their real *inner* origin instead of leaping to correct the outer causes these dark states always blame

For someone who is new to these ideas, these broad forms of self-study may sound not all that difficult to do. Actually, for an awake man or woman they are as natural "to do" spiritually as breathing is physically, but here we run into an interesting finding.

Most people believe that if they are physically awake, they are psychically awake as well. Perhaps they'll admit that until they've had their first cup of coffee in the morning they may not be too alert, but the rest of the time, they believe, they're fully conscious. However, this isn't the case! A trick of the mind keeps the deception going. Here's how it works. As soon as it's pointed out to us that we are not aware of ourselves, a TPIC sneaks in and snaps us into a kind of momentary wakefulness, wherein it's easy to believe we've been aware the entire time! This sort of self-awareness only lasts as long as the momentary challenge that produced it. For example, if someone were to ask you right now, "Are you aware of yourself?" you would become aware in the moment, and think that you always had been. But you were not, and in a few moments more you will forget this, and fall out of self-awareness once more. We would do well to consider carefully the words of Goethe, which serve both to remind and warn us: *"None are more hopelessly enslaved than those who falsely believe they are free."*

Here's another important thing to know. Nobody begins self-study as an "A" student. In fact, real self-study begins with becoming aware of just how unaware we really are. Don't let this last thought throw you! It's wise to see where our wisdom was only an assumption. This allows real wisdom, real self-knowledge, to grow. And this explains why some of our most important first lessons come when we set an exercise for ourselves, and later see that we altogether forgot about it. For example, when we realize, with a shock, that although we may have set a simple goal to watch out for a certain negative reaction in ourselves, many hours, or even days may have gone by without even one moment of seeing ourselves sink under its influence. Or perhaps we had decided to work on some small exercise in self-awareness at our place of employment. Maybe it was something as simple as just knowing our own facial expression when meeting with certain people for business. Now we're back home, sitting in our easy chair, when we suddenly remember we had dozens of face-wrenching encounters all day long and never remembered our exercise even once!

Bit by bit, a day at a time, it begins to dawn on us that we are generally lost in a fog of thought. Even as our aim to be self-studying reveals the fact of this inner fog, what comes with it is a whole new clarity about our inner condition; for now we can also see that the many things we've done that were thoughtlessly cruel or self-harming, we did only because we had been caught up in this same dazed state. We start to see that in this peculiar psychic sleep our priorities have been set by TPICs whose self-serving goals have only brought much frustration, or, at best, some temporary pleasure. Perhaps most important of all, we begin to learn that a larger world awaits us if we could but remember that reaching it requires staying awake enough to leave our smaller one behind.

Beginning to see that we're actually lost in thought all day is a valuable signal to us. It's equivalent to the doctor's diagnosis that is the necessary first step toward achieving a cure. We should never be discouraged by any discovery our self-study shows us. To be aware that we have been unaware is the beginning of real awareness. When increasing this kind of self-knowledge is our top priority, there can never be failure, but only new opportunities for growth. As we become increasingly aware of how we cause our own difficulties in our sleep state, we gain a new impetus to discover more about ourselves, to want something more from ourselves. And when this kind of inner wish is made sincerely and asked often enough, Reality itself steps in to make it come true. Surely, this understanding is part of what Scottish philosopher Thomas Carlyle intended to convey when he wrote:

> O thou that pinest in the imprisonment of the Actual, and criest bitterly to the gods for a kingdom wherein to rule and create, know this for a truth: the thing thou seekest is already here, 'here or nowhere,' couldst thou only see

New and True Benefits that Self-Study Brings

Often, when we first set out on the path of self-study, we begin with unrealistic or just plain mistaken expectations about what it will do for us. The unconscious wish that fuels this early stage of self-study is simply to become a better "old" person, rather than to become a completely new person.

Perhaps we have visions of suddenly becoming capable of handling easily any set of troublesome circumstances; or that our newly enlarged self-knowledge will enable us to control other people, or at least to no longer be bothered by what anyone does to us. We hope or believe that in this imagined self-mastery the universe will shower us with gifts such as money, relationships, and good fortune. Further, we may believe that these are the things we need to guarantee our future happiness. But can any of these exterior conditions deliver the inner contentment we want? No, they can't. See the following fact and let it reveal the path to higher and higher levels of inner freedom: even when these desires are fulfilled, they do nothing to expand the restricted world of *our self*. To the contrary, these trappings only tighten the secret grasp of the thought-self that now is strengthened in its belief in its own power. If we do what we call spiritual work for these "self"-ish reasons, we simply remain in our tiny world, seeking the ends that *that* world calls valuable. The only way out of that world is through self-study, which begins with showing us that devoting our lives to the never-ending agenda of never-satisfied TPICs will never lead us to lasting happiness.

When people approach their self-study with wrong expectations, they can quickly become discouraged when those expectations are not fulfilled. They then claim that self-study does not provide anything valuable in return for all the effort it requires, because it does not bring them what their minds tell them it should. Wanting only to feel good about themselves, according to their own worn-out ideas of what that means, they never enter into the realm of real self-study at all. Sadly, without knowing it, they close the door on a world that could have rewarded them beyond anything they even knew to ask for, which brings us to a surprising paradox along the path of self-study.

Guy tells us that the purpose of our inner investigation is not to feel pleased with ourselves—and certainly not to feel good about ourselves because of some new noble self-image as someone aiming to lead a better life. The true purpose of self-study is to invite something Good into our lives that then provides us with the unshakable Goodness we were previously unable to give ourselves.

We can only benefit from self-study when we use it correctly for self-discovery—and not just as one more ineffective attempt at self-creation. True self-study is not an exercise in confirming what has been, but an opening of ourselves to what is and to the always-becoming unknown. We can use it to illuminate the tiny world our false natures have held us captive in, allowing our discoveries to throw open the door to the larger world within that is our birthright.

Seek the Self-Knowledge that is Life's True Treasure

When it comes to our inner studies, it's possible to pass all the tests and still fail the course! What does this mean?

Concerted efforts to increase self-knowledge *can* lead to more effective behavior. We can indeed gain greater control over events as we gain greater perception into our own and others' motives. As a result, we pass many of life's tests with flying colors as we never could before, including developing greater confidence and being less dismayed by personal difficulties. But unless we go beyond what are essentially surface changes, all the way to defeating the intimate enemy, our improvements show themselves to be little more than a refinement of existing images; they are merely the addition of more controlled behaviors. In either case, it's still the old self trying to extract from its small world what it believes is valuable. We have "failed the course" because we have not learned the very real difference between being self-complacent and self-conquering. To illustrate the difference between this more common kind of self-control and the rewards of real self-change, Guy once gave the following example.

In this world, it's possible for you to find physical gold, but without winning the war within yourself, this wealth could not do anything for you other than perhaps produce a more comfortable place in which to continue your struggle with old conflicts. However, there is an inner gold you can find whose possession fulfills you, regardless of your external circumstances. We can call this inner gold "real self-knowledge": truths you know *about* your-self, *for* yourself and *from* yourself through your self-study. It's yours because you've visited the world where this new kind of gold exists; you've mined it yourself, and you've put it in your pocket. This gold can never be taken from you. Its Goodness is yours forever. This new inner wealth enriches you by transforming your very own ideas about who you are and what you really want from life. With it, everything gets simpler. And the nicest thing about this special Spiritual Gold is that you can have as much of it as you're willing to pay for.

On the other hand, and it warrants this short warning, *nothing* is as easy, and even secretly flattering as it can be, than to read certain books that build our self-images as being wise and "spiritual." These books, however, contain a subtle sort of spiritual "fool's gold" that keeps us trapped in an imaginary world. By contrast, real self-knowledge can be a little difficult to take at first, deliver-ing well-aimed blows to our vanity as it shows us how limited and artificial our self-created thought-world has been. But it also provides a glimpse of the expansive world that awaits us—if we will treasure the truth about ourselves that it alone can reveal. Amma Syncletica, one of the Desert Fathers, said:

> Great endeavors and hard struggles await those who are converted, but afterwards inexpressible joy. If you want to light a fire, you are troubled at first by smoke, and your eyes water. But in the end you achieve your aim. Now it is written: 'Our God is a consuming fire.' So we must light the divine fire in us with tears and struggle.

How to Achieve Your Heart's Desire

Just as it turned out to be for the young woman we met in the opening lines of this chapter, what we find in life is always a result of where we place our attention. If our heart longs to see a shooting star, that day will come when we'll see one blaze across the heavens. If we keep looking for physical gold, by panning a stream or breaking through rock, chances are our search will be rewarded, but when we seek the more valuable gold of real self-knowledge, we are guaranteed to find it. It is there in abundance just waiting to be uncovered. You can be assured of this new wealth of self if you add to your knowledge the forthcoming fact.

The most critical factor in determining *what* we find is *where* we place our attention. And whether understood or not at this point in your self-studies, we always place our attention on what we love.

An athlete will spend hours, day in and day out, perfecting his skill. A chess champion devotes her time and energy to refining her mental discipline. In the same fashion, if our true wish is to free ourselves from the clutches of the intimate enemy, then every moment is a new opportunity to practice the pursuit that ultimately leads to this priceless self-liberation.

Opportunities for self-study—and the changes these discoveries yield—present themselves endlessly, with new ones arriving with each new moment. The key point here is that if we don't undergo the changes within ourselves that we say we desire, it's because we are not awake to these unfolding opportunities. In other words, our attention is on something else. We are allowing ourselves to remain lost in the small world of the false nature and under the tyranny of its TPICs instead of watching ourselves within that world for the self-liberating lessons we can learn. It's easy to have our attention sidetracked in this way. The truth is that even though we may feel a strong pull in the direction of self-study, and long for the special freedom it alone can grant us, there also exists quite often an even stronger pull away from it. This is necessary knowledge and not to be discounted. Let us consider once more the words of St. Paul who spoke of this very same condition within himself. He told his students, "I don't do the Good I want to do, but instead the evil I don't want to do." He knew too well the hypnotic attractive power of the intimate enemy and how well it could make its desires seem his very own.

Constantly shaking ourselves into new self-awareness—and then struggling to snap out of the false self's gravitational field we find ourselves in—can be an exhausting experience; it's not unlike struggling to strip off a soaked, skin-tight sweatshirt. As long as we remain unaware of just how vulnerable we are to negative influences while asleep to ourselves, it seems easier to just remain in this psychic slumber. This is a state to which we have all grown accustomed, and the inertia that tends to keep us locked in it is very powerful. As a result, we're easily convinced that a little self-pampering is just what the doctor ordered!

"I don't feel up to working on myself today," we might hear ourselves say, or, "I'm too tired. Besides, there's no point in trying to quiet my mind when it's in such a whirl. I'll just wait for a better time when I'm more alert."

We must not fall under the power of these deceptive voices coming to us from within our own minds. We must refuse to accept that the weakness any TPIC claims as being ours is the same as our own. If we wait to do our self-study until we "feel like it," we'll never do it at all, for no TPIC ever wishes to be unmasked for the false guide it is. We must engage in the process of self-study as a *volitional* act, deliberately embarked upon regardless of whether we wish to or not. We cannot wait until we feel the time is right for self-work. Remember: when it comes to defeating the intimate enemy, "tomorrow's" victory never comes. Now is always the only time there is.

Touching again on an earlier idea in this chapter, it may be useful to think of self-study as a kind of health-giving spiritual prescription. When we suffer from a physical illness, we know we must take our medicine consistently, whether we want to or not, or we just won't get well. In the same way, we must do our self-study consistently, making efforts every day to observe ourselves in action. Just as the unhealthy person's urgent wish to recover his well-being helps him to overcome his resistance to taking the medicine that heals, so is it that our understanding of how unnecessarily painful our lives are when living only from our false selves eventually replaces our resistance to doing the necessary inner work.

Our resolve to live a Real Life is further strengthened when self-study reveals that at any moment we're not consciously in command of ourselves, something mechanical is in charge of us. In such a state of psychic sleep, we're vulnerable to be taken over by whatever TPIC may appear to run the show. Of even greater significance is that each time we give ourselves over to yet another unconscious response, we lose that precious opportunity to close the curtain, for good, on the whole act of the intimate enemy.

Make Your Escape to a Better Life with Self-Study

When we think about our lives, it is clear that we do the same things every day. We get ready in the morning. We eat a meal. Perhaps we go shopping. With such repetition, it's no time at all before everything about our lives becomes routine.

Where's the renewal in any repeated action performed unconsciously? Where's the fun in just eating again? Sure, it may be pleasurable, but with self-study we can do something more than just trying to please ourselves over and over again in the same old way. We can set an aim to watch ourselves during every seemingly familiar act, and see what delightful new adventures our watchfulness brings us to.

Self-study adds a whole new dimension to our daily experience. Remembering to observe ourselves as often as we can, we are then open to discovering one new world after another—both within ourselves and in the world going on around us. Even the most superficial encounter with others places us in a potential gold mine if we can remember to stay awake and watchful of ourselves and friends.

For example, today we can make an exercise to stay awake during our social gatherings just to see if any one topic of conversation is ever completed. Of course, very few ever are, because each of the participants unconsciously redirects the conversation, drawing upon something occurring within his or her own immediate world. In coming awake to this peculiar psychological phenomenon we don't try to change other people's behavior, or even to point out the endless pointlessness in such meandering talk. We do learn, however, how it is that we continually find ourselves off track. And once this trick of the TPIC is made clear, so is the secret of how we can keep ourselves on a single, more successful life course.

It's easy to find especially fruitful areas in which to work at self-study. For one case in point, we all take part in certain activities every day more likely to lull us into a state of psychic sleep. Maybe it's talking on the phone with a friend, or watching TV. Once we've identified these behaviors, we can make an extra effort to shake ourselves awake and fight against being pulled under. For best success, find out for yourself those times and conditions where you're most likely to fall asleep to yourself. For example, while watching TV or a movie, make an aim to notice how much your emotional strings are pulled by the kind of music that's underscoring the scene. You might even turn the show off altogether for a few minutes, right in the middle of a moving moment, just to see how that makes you feel! Here's the point: find those places where you most tend to fall asleep, and work there![1]

When we shake ourselves awake in this way, by consciously stepping outside of any given event, what we're given to see is that all we've really done is step outside of the stream of our own thoughts. This mental or emotional stream is the only force that ever carries us away! Gratefully, we discover that the more we practice freeing ourselves in this way, the freer we become. What a great day it is when instead of seeing every event in the way the intimate enemy wants us to see it, we begin to use those same events to escape its small world. Little by little it dawns on us that everything about this life is an opportunity for self-study! Now we have something new to do every moment. Even taking a walk is no longer just a walk; it's a journey of self-discovery.

Whatever we do, we can consciously create new ways to watch ourselves and with each attempt become more aware of the restrictive self-created world in which we habitually mentally dwell. When we see that world as it really is, we no longer want to stand within the stream of its painful thoughts and memories. We want to be more constant residents of the larger world of Reality, and be what Truth wants us to be. And so our attention is always focused on sighting those shooting stars of self-revelation that guide us further forward toward that new life we know we are meant to experience.

1. For those readers who want to take the next step to work with specific exercises in self-study, read Guy's book *Designing Your Own Destiny*. The body of this book consists of eleven inner-life exercises designed specifically to help the reader reach new and Higher levels of self-awareness.—E.B.D.

Four Insights that Guarantee Self-Success

Too often it happens that some people lose their interest in self-study. They give up on their inner work because they don't see the immediate results hoped for. If anything, in their growing awareness of what has always been their actual condition, it seems to them that they are now even deeper asleep than ever before! Don't fall for this trick! The negative thoughts urging you to cease your self-exploration come only from the mind of the intimate enemy. It knows that *your* persistent inner work is the same as *its* walking papers. The only weapon this false self has is its power of discouragement. So don't listen! Instead, be encouraged by the fact that although you will likely fail many times along the upper path, self-study and inner success are really two ideas that mean the same thing, if you'll only stay the course. All you have to do to stay the course and to win the inner war is be willing to start over and over and over again with your self-study. And here we encounter another beautiful law of higher life created just to help us succeed:

Starting over is *always* possible because Now is always *new.*

Life is continuously new in the present moment, *and so are you*. The negative voices issued from the intimate enemy that proclaim you won't make it come only from what has been your world up until now, and not from Life in its perpetual newness. Seeing the truth of this gives you the strength to brush away these feelings of failure and start over with self-study.

To double their inner benefit, read and then reread the following four special insights that Guy offers on this vital subject of self-study and the importance of starting over.

1.   The power to start over is in the thread of reality itself. Volunteer to view every unhappy ending or defeat as the continually passing condition it is. Real self-study proves to you that there's no such thing as defeat, for the voice that tells of your defeat is itself only an echo of a time that was. What was is no more unless you allow the intimate enemy to convince you that an echo is reality.

2.   All feelings of failure include the unconscious assumption that you know all there is to know about what has you bottled up. Pull the plug on this self-limitation by meeting every moment of self-defeat with the realization that there's no end to your ability to learn about yourself.

3.   Just as the physical eye that sees can't see itself other than through a reflection, you cannot see your psychological self other than by gazing at those mental images of your own creation. So, when seeing a failure in your mind's eye, just remember in that moment who it is that put it there. See through the painful feeling by seeing its root as arising from within your conditioned self. Seeing that you unconsciously put that picture on the screen begins the inner healing that only real self-knowledge can provide.

4. Each moment that some self-study shows you how
    spiritually asleep you are, use that same moment
    to wake up and remember that you can always
    start your whole life over. Then see that the inner
    voice calling you a loser should be the focus of still
    a deeper self-study, and not the self that you look
    at yourself from.

Let the Light Fight for You

The truths we uncover through self-study gradually strip
away all of our false self-conceptions, those mistaken
ideas and beliefs about ourselves that have kept us in a
war within the world of our own conditioned thought.
Clearly, we can't advance on the inner path if we believe
our thoughts can and must determine for us where that
path will take us. The beginning of the real path starts
when we see there is no path where we always sought it
in our own minds. This knowledge is revealed to us
through self-study. The Truth wants to guide us, but it
can't do so when we have layer upon layer of misconcep-
tions in the way, blocking out that still small, but higher,
voice. That's why the purpose of self-study is not to build
what our own thoughts tell us is right for us, but to
detect and reject everything that's wrong.

Self-study truly is the royal road to the Higher Self
bringing with it many thrilling discoveries, moments of
joy, and new energy and enthusiasm for life. But arriving
at these higher experiences takes consistent effort in the
face of setbacks, confusion, and even at times what feels

like real loss. However, be assured, nothing real can ever be lost any more than the light of the sun can be outshone by the moon. There is an order to all things, and self-study is the light that reveals all shadowy selves for what they are. Here is the hidden meaning behind the ancient idea of letting the Light fight for you. Let it.

Special Summary

> . . . we must begin where we begin, and put away any other concerns about where that beginning is. It's enough just to make a start, wherever that may be. What difference does it make at what point you enter into a great river? Sooner or later, all its waters reach and pour into the sea.
>
> Never let discouragement have the final word and one day there will be nothing left to discuss. Besides, you can have just as many new beginnings as you're willing to leave behind all your ideas about yourself. Nothing in this world, or in any other, can stop you from discovering your Original, Free Being. This has always been your destiny . . .

— Guy Finley
Designing Your Own Destiny

9

> *When we first seek the truth, we think
> we are far from it. When we discover
> that the truth is already in us, we are all
> at once our original self.*

— Dogen

THE FREEDOM OF LIVING IN THE FIRST PERSON

Imagine it's Friday afternoon . . . in midsummer . . . in New York City. The Manhattan streets teem with people rushing by us, but we are invisible witnesses, undetected inner-life detectives! We can focus on any one of them at will, and we select as our first object of study a gentleman who is rushing down Wall Street.

Here's a distinctive-looking man about to complete a huge arbitrage deal, and it's essential that he sign certain papers before the banks close for the weekend. The expression on his face and the posture of his body as he rapidly weaves his way through the crowd clearly reveal his sense of self-importance and purpose. This is a man whose every movement advertises his belief that victory is within his grasp.

Leaving the financier to carry out his business, we seek out our next subject, and arrive at the rooftop of an exclusive health resort. High above the noise of the city streets, we find ourselves in a little oasis with potted trees and an inviting pool fed by a melodious waterfall. A wealthy matron reclines in one of the chaise lounges, eyes hidden behind sunglasses, hair wrapped in a turban, face covered in cucumbers, and a slightly lost expression around the mouth.

Back in the streets once more, we enter a dingy cafe, way off on one of the side streets in a row of badly run-down buildings. A middle-aged man sits on one of the stools, dejectedly staring down at his half-eaten sandwich, hardly noticing the tray of dirty dishes sitting on the counter to his right.

We've looked into the lives of three seemingly very different people, and yet all share a common secret, an underlying psychic feature they all feel that greatly determines why they are doing what they do in any given moment. But these three are not alone with their secret. The truth is most men and women carry the weight of it, without ever seeing the fact of their invisible burden. For now, returning to the three people in our example, their life secret, which even they don't know, is that they behave as they do, and seek what they seek, because they feel cut off.

The man running to the bank hopes that if he makes enough money this time he will finally have that permanent sense of confidence and accomplishment he seeks. He will know himself to be a major actor at the center of things, and will at last have something solid under his feet that can't be taken away.

The woman at the health club also senses that something essential is missing from her life. She hopes that perhaps the right new beauty treatment or aerobic exercise will restore her feelings of youth and promise, and make her feel it is not too late for her to see the fulfillment of her most heartfelt dreams.

The man in the cafe just feels lost and isolated—betrayed by a world that he says has kept him from becoming all that he was intended to be. Unwilling at the moment to reenter the battlefield where he has suffered so many defeats, he is just passing time at the lunch counter where, nursing his resentments, he searches his memory for something or someone to blame for his seemingly hopeless station in life.

Look around you, wherever you may be and at any moment. Try to see through the roles of actors and actresses crossing this or that stage of life; look past their appearances and seeming differences and you'll find all share one thing in common: people do the things they do in order to try and provide themselves with a feeling of being complete. They sense that there is a great gap in their lives. More to the point: they feel cut off. And it's true, we are cut off. The reason why we remain this way, despite all the money we make, or the trips we take, and all the other things we do to resolve the nagging psychological discomfort we feel, is because we don't know what it is we're cut off from! And we don't understand in what way we are cut off. We just know at a deep, unconscious level that we too often feel isolated and incomplete.

Not knowing the true cause of our lost feelings, we seek our own explanation. Instead of saying, "I feel cut off," we say, "I feel poor," or, "I feel afraid," or, "I feel left out and lonely." Each of these perceived problems brings its own solution. "Make more money." "Convince people to see me as an authority." "Get even with those cruel people who have caused me so much pain." And if none of these work, "Feel dejected over this personal failure, or this increased evidence of the world's insensitivity."

So we pursue these solutions that we've offered ourselves, but none of them brings the ultimate sense of completion we desire. They cannot, because the problem does not lie in the state of our finances or our relationships with others. It does not lie in the way our parents treated us or the way the government runs things. And all our endeavors to fix our problems that are directed toward these areas do nothing to get at the root of our unhappiness. The pain we feel at any time, no matter what we believe to be the cause, is due only to the fact that we are indeed cut off from knowing our connection with the True Source of our own lives. We do not feel ourselves to be an essential part of the world around us, receiving energy and direction from something higher. Instead, we feel at enmity with life, forced to make our way, to prove ourselves, to provide for ourselves a sense of wholeness and completion.

We're like the poor man who has been invited to stay in the castle of a great king. Not realizing he is a welcome guest, and thinking he must continue to fend for himself, he steals scraps of food from the kitchen, which never satisfy him. His failure to understand his true status prevents him from seeing the huge banquet that is generously spread for him in the dining room, where he can take as much as he wishes. Unable to see the bounty that awaits him, he may even blame the good king for treating him so cruelly!

So, what is it that blocks us from seeing the fullness of life that surrounds us on every side?

Yes, that's right. It is the intimate enemy that first isolates us and that then engages us, continually, on an imaginary battlefield. The false nature immediately jumps in at every new moment to impose its distorted interpretation on every event, to judge in terms of its notion of how things should be. Before anything new or spontaneous in us can experience life directly and understand things in a fresh, new light, something old and mechanical intercedes to protect us—not who we truly are, but who it perceives itself to be. As each TPIC arises, it turns in upon itself to give a sense of wholeness to its momentary, fictitious world; to give itself a sense of completion; and in doing so it cuts us off from Life itself! From years past the words of author George Macdonald confirm what must be done: "All the doors that lead inward to the secret place of the most high are doors outward; out of the self—out of smallness—out of wrong."

Taking Charge of the Temporary Person in Charge

At any moment, the TPIC convinces us that its world view is the correct one, and the only possible one. To break free of its control, we have to catch it in the act of twisting our view of life to make it conform to its needs for self-perpetuation. By catching it in this way, we gain insight into how the TPIC cuts us off from the larger world of Reality. Catching the TPIC is not easy, for until now we have been convinced that each TPIC is who we really are. If we know how to use everyday situations and other people for our own education, however, the opportunities for our enlightenment are endless. For example, we've already looked at how learning to sit back and watch ourselves and others in conversation can be a fruitful area of study. Now let's look a little more deeply into this simple exercise and see what other possibilities for self-revelation these encounters with others can provide.

We can learn to use other people for our own spiritual gain by watching them to see what they do and using their behavior as a mirror to our own. Our observations of them allow us to see what it is that we do, and therefore help us to understand why we feel as we feel. What wonderful lessons we can learn if we will watch and do our inner work all the time and with everyone.

Here is one particular behavior you can watch when you're with other people that can reveal much about why and how we feel cut off. When you're with a group of friends or associates, perhaps enjoying a casual conversation during a meal, observe how each person present turns everything that is said in on himself. One person cannot utter a sentence without it being picked up and altered into what another person knows about the topic, no matter how tortured or distant that connection may be! She mentions a great recipe for clam chowder, and he jumps in commenting that the best clam chowder he ever had was in Boston. Then the next five minutes are centered on his last visit to that city! We are all experts on the topic of ourselves, and given the smallest opening we will turn everything into an opportunity to expound on that topic. People do not talk to one another; they talk to themselves. No matter what topic they bring up, it is really about themselves. When others twist that topic to fit their own needs, the originator of the topic gets irritated. And each time people turn the topic to themselves, or feel annoyed because the topic has been turned away from them, they cut themselves off.

Our observations of this behavior reveal to us that it is the nature of the false self to be self-centered. It cannot exist apart from the nucleus of its experience, and so it grasps at every opening to describe and relive that experience. Everything must revolve around the nucleus of the TPIC of the moment, or that particular TPIC comes apart, which it frequently does. But that breaking up of a TPIC is not a problem for the larger nucleus of the false self. A TPIC is only one soldier in the war. The intimate enemy has many more in its legion to send forth. So perhaps one TPIC unsuccessfully tries to turn the conversation to itself. Its failure causes it to come apart, but it is replaced instantaneously by an irritated TPIC that provides a new center the person can turn in on, and therefore know himself or herself once more.

As a result of the fact that it is usually TPICs who converse, and not individuals genuinely interacting with one another, there is rarely any real communication. The word *communication* has as its root "commune," which can be understood as non-interfering, interrelating energies, but TPICs are, at their basis, interfering energies. We're cut off because TPICs are always making efforts to feel filled and "plugged in," and it is those very efforts that secretly cut us off. Each TPIC in its turn convinces us that if we succeed in making it feel permanent, we will feel permanent, and we fall for it every time because we don't know that what we are really cut off from has nothing to do with any TPIC's formula for happiness and success.

We mistakenly believe that we're cut off from a feeling of approval, or a feeling of well-being we could derive from possessing things. We compound the error by believing that if we could just fill in that gap, we would feel right ourselves. However, what it is that we're truly cut off from is not anything that any thought or emotion can name. And the more we seek satisfaction by turning in on ourselves in an attempt to complete the circle as the TPIC demands, the more cut off we feel. Sometimes the TPIC's prescribed behavior is successful. We experience a temporary victory, and in a sense are "turned on." Sometimes it is not successful, and we turn on ourselves. In either case, some aspect of the false self is confirmed, and the True Self is further buried within a circle of thought that blocks it from meeting life directly. As we see more and more how each one of our own attempts to make ourselves feel complete leaves us feeling empty and searching again, we gain the power to refuse to take the TPIC's lead. As we do so, the false structure of the self begins to collapse. As each suffocating layer falls away, something real emerges that experiences life in a new way.

Find the Magic of the Original Moment

For one of our August meetings, Guy suggested we do something different: we would leave behind our usual meeting room, and instead hold our discussion in a nearby park. As we gathered in this natural setting next to the Rogue River, we sensed we would hear something special this morning, something that would pull us further out of our old selves. Indeed, in his talk Guy showed us quite clearly the difference between the enclosed world of thought in which we usually dwell and the open universe that lies beyond ourselves. He began his talk with a play on the words of a popularly known phrase, "there's more to reality than meets the eye," by telling us, "There's more to reality than meets the 'I.' " In other words, he was saying that those experiences that we habitually see as our "normal" lives exist within an already larger universe that is largely unseen; learning to stay awake within ourselves is the same as having the opportunity to glimpse a new and expanded reality whose new view naturally lifts us up and out of our presently limited ideas about who we are. Guy then proceeded to tell us of a special insight he had received one morning while eating watermelon!

At first, several of us thought that he was just having some lighthearted fun—as we often do at points in our discussions about the higher life. However, the next moment it was clear that we were about to embark on an important study-lesson, when he asked if any of us had ever really considered all the secret spiritual lessons—the miracle—existing in any piece of fruit! Just think about this question for yourself. As you're about to see, there's more to it than meets either the eye, or the "I"!

Watermelon juice is sweet. Lemon juice is sour. Yet, they're both water. Why is one sweet and one sour? What makes each of them water with a different quality? Something in the seed of each fruit instructs the plant to take something different from the ground and to process it in a different way. What was the intelligence that decided that? In what way does that intelligence act in our own lives? If you'll ask yourself these simple questions, as we were ourselves asked to do that bright August morning, you too will start to see a whole new world right where you are; a world that is open and orderly; an invisible world of Wisdom at work all around you, revealed in all things physical, yet hardly noticed by anyone. And if we can see the beauty in this unseen world which patiently awaits our conscious entrance, then we must also ask ourselves the next question: When it's given to us to be ever-renewed explorers of higher and higher worlds right within our own, why then do we spend so much time thinking about so many proven worthless, self-torment-ing, self-enclosing things?

The truth here is troubling to those self-pleasing pictures we all have of ourselves, but results reveal the rule: we are not awake in our own life experience. The miracles are missed because we, ourselves, are missing.

Bound up as we are within the closed world of our own TPICs, we see virtually nothing other than what the false self of the moment wants for us to see. We miss the miracles around us—and lose their vital life lessons in the process. What are intended to be our new experiences are taken in and twisted by the TPIC's interpretation, turned into something familiar that it knows how to deal with. And its interpretations are always some variation on a past theme dished out again in one form or another. Can you begin to see what going through life in this way does to our daily experience? It fills us with an often unconscious but continuous feeling of deep boredom—better known in these sadly sarcastic times as the "Been there— Done that!" syndrome. Do you recognize the diagnosis?

The new car, the new relationship, the trip, the beautiful day: the enjoyment of all is marred by the unconscious reaction that "I've been through that." People go to extremes seeking new thrills, believing the spontaneity and real pleasure they seek will be found in the next activity. They never realize that no matter what they do it can never be new, because that which experiences the event within them is mechanical and old, twisting everything new into what has already been.

By contrast, in real life, everything is an original. Think back to a time you might have spent in a park, at the seashore, in a garden. What is it about a natural setting that makes it splendid and sacred, that gives rise to feelings of pleasure? For example, think about the sound of a stream. What is it that makes it nice? Why do we find it always refreshing? It's because a river never sounds the same way twice. It's the same wherever we look in nature. Every moment is an original moment. And within the world of nature, we see nothing but originals. No pine tree is exactly like any other. No sparrow is the same as any other sparrow. Even bird songs, while they have recognizable patterns, are never repeated in exactly the same way. Why is it that in a world that is continually new, we ourselves do not experience a continual sense of newness? It is because we do not meet this newness with something that is new in us, alive in the present moment. We do not experience life directly. Instead, it is one TPIC or another that meets life for us. And since the TPIC itself is a product of memory, and interprets everything to fit its memory-produced momentary purpose, the world we experience becomes repetitious and old.

It is possible, in fact we are intended, to live in what Guy calls the "first person." We are born with a nature that is as new as each original moment and that always meets this new moment for the first time. The life experiences that pass easily through this new nature are themselves always new. They are not a creation of any past experience, which means each is incomparable. Because of this special state, none are ever found to be wanting. This free Original Self that experiences everything directly is in communion with life, for it does not interfere with it or wish it to be different. It does not seek to capture an identity in any event, for living in harmony with the fullness of life, it already has everything it needs. It does not turn in on itself to find completion, and therefore does not ensnare itself in a world that, by its own fragmentary nature, must always be incomplete and cut off. Compare this self with the sad state of affairs surrounding the un-life of the TPIC and it should be clear: We can only be happy when we live in the first person.

How can we free ourselves of these TPICs and come to live this direct life in the first person? It is by catching ourselves each time a TPIC is about to turn in on itself, and instead, open the circle.

Stepping Outside the Circle of Self

Many of the passages and parables in the great sacred texts, when studied for their higher lessons, provide us with a road map for the inner journey. One particular passage from the New Testament is especially valuable in helping us to understand what it means to open the circle. This frequently misunderstood passage tells us:

> Whatsoever you shall bind on earth, the same you shall bind in Heaven, and whatsoever you shall loose on earth, the same shall be loosed in Heaven.

The deeper meaning of these words becomes more clear to us as we return to the original Aramaic in which Christ spoke. Due to the richness of this ancient language, words had layers of meaning that enriched the inner lesson, but that have been lost in modern-day translations. In Aramaic, the words *to bind* and *to loose* were connected to one another, and both of them had to do with the distribution of energy. To bind meant to cause something to become enmeshed by enclosing lines of energy. The word implied a process of closing something down. Its opposite, to loosen, referred to the liberation of energy through the process of opening something up.

This energy that could be bound or loosed is the force of Life itself, which is intended to descend from Heaven, animate the individual, and then reascend into Heaven in one continuous free flow. This energy connected the higher to the lower, so that human life on earth was perpetually inspired and directed from above. There was no disconnection between Heaven and man. Human life was complete and ever new because it was a continuous reflection of the whole universe in its always original moment.

The binding of this energy occurred within the individual who, through identification and attachments, enmeshed it within the self. As a result of this process of turning in, the circle of energy exchange was broken. The individual was cut off, and the energy that was—in this way—bound on earth could not return to its source; therefore it was also bound in Heaven. To loose on earth meant to loosen, or liberate, that once-bound energy. By opening the circle, the energy could now return, and therefore could be loosed in Heaven.

All of this relates absolutely to everything we have been saying about the TPICs and how they interfere with our direct experience of life. Turning in upon ourselves is the same as closing the circle of self. Whether we're criticizing ourselves or applauding ourselves, each time we turn in we're cutting ourselves off. Our misguided thoughts tell us we're completing the circle by latching onto an identity and making ourselves feel real, but our continuing feelings of being lost prove to us that we are, in reality, only isolating ourselves by our unconscious actions. Every time we turn the conversation to the desires of the TPIC, instead of experiencing the fullness of the moment and the people in it, we're cutting ourselves off. Every time we pursue a goal that our minds tell us will make us feel right about ourselves in its fulfillment, and we forget that in the higher world everything has already been achieved for us, we're cutting ourselves off. As Henry Van Dyke observed: "Self is the only prison that can ever bind the soul." The unenlightened individual is always turning it in, but those of us who wish to experience a Higher life must learn to turn it loose.

We have countless opportunities every day to loosen something on earth, to open the circle of energy, so it can be loosed in Heaven. Instead, we bind energy. For example, perhaps you meet a friend on the street. Stopping to chat, you attempt to direct every aspect of your interaction to fulfill your own self-centered goals, and in so doing you turn in on yourself. As you walk away, you think about the conversation and judge yourself as having performed well or poorly, and all the time you're binding even more energy within your small circle of self.

Or perhaps you try to meditate, and instead of opening yourself to the unknown by letting go of your ideas of what it is to meditate, you sink into imaginary ideas about what you're supposed to think and feel, and so you close up the circle once more.

The only cure for this self-imposed isolation is to loosen ourselves, to release ourselves from the circle of self. What we are releasing are the energies that we have, in the past, only known to turn in for a sense of self-completion, which has really been a cutting off of the self from everything true, good, and Everlasting.

This deep, life-healing explanation amounts to nothing but words for those who have never caught themselves in the act of turning in, who have never been awake to the exact moment when the energy is bound and the cutting off begins. If we are alert, however, we can watch the process as it happens, and thereby gain a deeper understanding of how we come to be so frequently lost within the small world of the self. When our observation of the process enables us to halt its flow, and we feel ourselves actually shaking loose the unpleasant feelings, we are motivated to seek additional self-revelations. Here is a small example of an experience I had that clarified the entire process to me.

One afternoon, I was driving out of a parking lot when a flurry of traffic and a driver who turned unexpectedly almost caused an accident. Fortunately, nothing serious happened, but as I continued on my way, my thoughts focused on the event. I was still anxious about the narrowly averted accident, and sought to blame the other driver. At that point, there occurred what was truly a miracle in the deepest sense of the word. I suddenly recalled Guy's class lesson from the night before and the exercise he gave us to "turn it loose." That recollection caused me to become aware of myself. My observations showed me very clearly that I was in the process of shutting myself up into the world my thoughts were creating about the event. A TPIC had popped up to interpret the circumstance, and it was now content to relive it again and again. It was as though I could actually see the thoughts circling around, just as spiraling winds begin to create a storm system. My pause enabled me to catch my thoughts in the act of turning in; I experienced the resulting churning emotions, and saw how my awareness of the world around me was growing more and more limited.

Then, I followed this new voice that had shaken me into awareness and prompted me to turn it loose. It was as though I could feel a circle of energy opening to something above and beyond my present state of consciousness. I shook off the shell that had been tightening about me, and broke free to the larger world. Once I had done so, it became obvious that there had never been a need for me to get lost in that small world at all. The person who had almost had an accident was gone within a split second after the event was over. She was no more than a figment of imagination in the present moment, and had no right to dominate my life with these completely unnecessary fears and repeating images. Only who I really was in that moment, a conscious, ever-becoming being had the right to be in that moment.

How many times during any day does an event evoke a TPIC that then gathers thoughts and energy to it, and turns in to create a limited, imprisoned self? How many times do we miss the opportunity to catch this process, stop it in mid-step, and break out? Each time we fall for the TPIC's trick of turning in, we are removed from real life. Each time we break free, we give ourselves the chance of living life in the first person.

It may sound too simple, but the truest things in life usually are. The secret of winning a new life is to refuse to turn in on yourself. Instead, turn it loose. Turn loose your despair, your fear, your false excitement. Turn loose the self-image that seeks to entrench itself in the moment and take temporary control. Open up the circle. The false self wants to turn in, so it can close the circle and make itself feel complete. That's all it knows to do. Its goal is to perpetuate itself. The antidote is to turn it loose.

Turning it loose means becoming aware that we're cutting ourselves off each time we turn in, and then, when the challenge comes, to refuse to do it. Each time we turn it loose, we find ourselves psychologically floating in a kind of unknown space, uncertain who we are supposed to be in that moment. These new sensations may be disconcerting at first, but then it dawns on us that this is an experience to savor. When we no longer live an artificial life by living within the self-created world our own minds produce, we are free to experience ourselves and life as we and it really are. In the fullness of that first person original moment, we no longer feel cut off.

How to Release Yourself from Yourself

It is critical to our inner transformation that we take advantage of every opportunity to keep from turning in.

The intimate enemy wants to cut us off from real life and keep us battling within the small, encircled world that it creates. Only in this way can it perpetuate itself. Sometimes, the world in which it closes us up doesn't feel like a battlefield. Sometimes it feels like a playground, or a victory celebration, but it is always temporary. It always leads to ultimate disappointment, and it always leaves us feeling cut off.

In the past we didn't know that we could refuse to follow the TPIC onto the battlefield, and so we always went. Now we are learning that the entire battlefield is a fiction that we can avoid altogether—if we are alert at the critical moment so we can keep from being drawn in. This is a special spiritual skill that can and must be developed. Every part of our conditioned selves does not want us to do so. It has no taste for first person experience. It wants everything to remain familiar. When it feels that things are happening as they should it feels comfortable and in control. And if things are not happening as they should, a TPIC pops up that can feel betrayed or puzzled. Either way is fine with the false nature, as long as some aspect of itself is meeting and knowing itself through evaluating the event.

By deliberately creating conditions that increase our awareness, we begin to experience life directly, without the intercedence of the false nature. Of course, each of us must ultimately create our own situations in which this self-liberating experience can occur, but Guy suggests a number of exercises we can do that will place us in situations where the mind cannot rush in with its usual answers. By performing any of these, we increase our opportunities for seeing what it means to live in the first person:

1. Look for and enter into unfamiliar conditions that have the power to challenge you psychologically or emotionally. Hundreds of these opportunities present themselves every day. For example, instead of sleeping in until the time when you usually get up, get out of bed at the moment you awaken in the morning. The sleepy TPIC wants to wait for the alarm to sound or for the hands on the clock to read a certain hour. It doesn't want the shock of having to face the world without a prepared agenda. The first person experience is to face the day at an unaccustomed hour, to become aware of the different quality of the light and the unusual sounds. A part of you that always savors going back to sleep is already complaining, "But I won't like it." At first, maybe you won't, but this is not the point! The real point here is that the you that says it won't like it isn't the real you. It's the false self. Your goal is to detect and reject this second-hand person, which gets easier and easier to do as you see that there is never anything new in its second-hand life.

2. Sit quietly by yourself, secluded from all forms of stimulation. Don't let yourself go to sleep. Don't even meditate. Simply sit there with nothing familiar to do or hang on to, and become aware of how something inside of you keeps telling you to do

something or tries to pull you off on one thought-path or another. Each time you realize that your thoughts have wandered, bring yourself back into the present moment. Become aware of how different it feels to be separated from everything that normally tells you who you are. You're coming face to face with yourself. Now, don't make the mistake of imagining the "spiritual" person you think you should be seeing. Face yourself as you are. To become aware of this self stripped of all its usual forms of identity is a first person experience that can be the first step to breaking through to a whole new world.

3. Deliberately drop one cherished idea and meet life without it. For example, refuse to judge another's behavior as you normally would. Usually, we approach every experience with a basket full of expectations and demands. Then, regardless of whether or not they are met, we know what to do. If they are met we feel justified; if they are not we have an excuse to be angry or upset. In this exercise, we work within ourselves to drop all expectations and demands regarding other people's behavior. We simply observe what they do, and make no personalized judgment as to the value or meaning of their actions. By doing this, we take away any excuse of a TPIC to turn in and get an identity through others' behavior. If we fail at this and realize we've made the judgment anyway, our new

awareness shows us how harmful these judgments have always been to ourselves and others. As a result, every interaction becomes a first person experience, and the beneficial effect of this on all your relationships may surprise you!

4. Attempt to spend one whole day when the only time you speak is when spoken to. As your initial reaction to this must have already told you, this can be very difficult to do. Our discomfort at even thinking about doing this proves what we've been saying all along: an important aspect of all our interactions is our attempt to use them to turn in on ourselves and reinforce an identity. As we watch how we feel when we attempt to wait until spoken to, we are clearly shown that our conversation has always been self-serving. We also become aware of other people, whom we now really listen to for perhaps the first time. When a familiar TPIC does not jump forward to meet the moment, something else will be there, something truly compassionate and wise in all interactions. Then all meetings will be new because they will be a first person experience.

5. If you have a task to do that can be completed in either five steps or one, take the longer way. If you do, a familiar TPIC will complain about how stupid this is. After all, you have more important things to do. What if someone sees you being so foolish? Really listen to what these voices are say-

ing. Is what they want you to do really more important than developing the awareness of your own higher self-consciousness that this exercise is designed to produce? What is it in you that is always in a hurry to get things done? Where is it going? Has it ever gotten "there" and remained at the rest it rushed to reach? Challenge this self and you'll encounter feelings you've never known. Here's another door to a first person experience!

These exercises lead us to a whole new universe of self-understanding. However, their many benefits may be overshadowed at first because they can make us feel uncomfortable.

That's just the point! We are uncomfortable anyway. The TPICs just have us so turned in all the time that our mental fog prevents our awareness of the discomfort. These exercises give us an opportunity to see that our self-images are not real and have no power to help us when we're thrown into a new situation. We also see that when we get over our discomfort, life without the TPICs really is okay. In fact, it's better than okay. We taste a different kind of experience. We begin to sense the benefits of opening the circle of self. With practice, our ability to drop the TPIC that wants us to turn in increases. We find ourselves opening the circle more and more. In this growing state of openness, we feel that we are opening the channel to that Higher energy source that lifts our lives to a new level. And when this happens, we realize that this was the true purpose of our lives all along.

Your Final Victory over the
Intimate Enemy

In this part of the book, and all those that have preceded
it, we have raised and discussed many new ideas that
you may have never considered before. Higher ideas
such as these do not become your life's helpful partner
just by reading them. It doesn't work that way. As everything in this book proclaims, you must learn the truth of
them from yourself. If they are to come alive for you, it
must occur within you and through your own life experience. This is why so many inner exercises have been
provided for you. Each one provides you with a whole
new way to "know thyself"—revealing new opportunities
one after another to discover for yourself whether the
facts about your life and the intimate enemy are indeed
as they've been described over the course of these last
nine chapters.

Perhaps the main idea connected to your self-investigation is that something lives within you that calls itself
your friend, counselor, and guide. It speaks with your
voice and you "hear" it say with your own ears that it is
who you are. But in fact this self is not you. It is nothing
more than a collection of conditioned responses and
mechanical reactions, some of which came with this
machinery called your body, and some learned through
life's many divergent experiences. We have called this collection that constitutes your false self "the intimate
enemy." Like any collection, the intimate enemy is a bun-
dle of fragments, each of which is incomplete. This psy-

chic nature doesn't even speak with a single voice, but through a number of "selves" that have developed over time to deal with different types of situations. We've called each of these incomplete "selves" the Temporary Person in Charge, or TPIC: a momentary self, itself but a creation of the moment which produces the conditions for its brief appearance.

It is not that this newly revealed false nature serves no purpose at all. In fact, far from being harmful, certain of its aspects are natural and necessary for our own practical interaction with the physical world. In certain respects, this false nature is similar to Freud's concept of the ego. Freud looked upon the ego as a complex mechanical structure (although he likened it to a callous) that developed at the interface between the self and the physical world. He considered that the ego was really formulated to be a servant to the self.

The problem with this false self that makes it the intimate enemy is that it has taken control of the self! Instead of being a good servant, it becomes master, and a bad one at that! In the darkness of this unconscious reversal of Reality is induced a kind of psychic slumber in which the real conscious self, like the Sleeping Beauty in the fairy tale, drowses behind a wall of thorns. The servants have taken control of kingdom and castle, while the true monarch remains unknown. This is our actual condition: cut off from real life lying just beyond the obscuring wall of self. The point of our self-investigation and inner work is to rouse the sleeping monarch latent in each of us so it can take rightful control.

"But," you may well ask, "who is it that does this inner work?"

Fortunately, in some people, there exist a few right servants who sense there's no future for them in the craziness of the kingdom and castle where they find themselves living. They throw their lot in with the sleeping monarch whom they labor to awaken. Most likely, it's one of these right and loyal servants in you who is reading this book right now, and who, encouraged by these reinforcing facts, is inspired anew to continue with his or her sacred effort. When the true monarch awakens, that right servant will be rewarded, for this act of conscious self-sacrifice has granted him or her a whole new life—a real life—the rightful life.

As we apply ourselves to this special inner work of self-awakening we may find yet new worries; distant but distinct concerns about what will happen to us if we persist with our efforts to free ourselves from our selves.

Who will we be? Who will do all the necessary things that must be done? Will we still remember how to bake an apple pie or fix a carburetor? Will we have to give up "this" or "that" which we still love, but suspect is really self-defeating? Please heed reality's reply: all self-concerns such as these are unnecessary.

On the surface, you and your life will continue to look pretty much the same to everyone in the world who doesn't know anything of your inner work. Yes, you may seem calmer than the average person. More than likely, you won't get involved in petty conversations as you did before. Your relationships will improve. Still, the fact is that this false nature of ours is not meant to completely disappear. It just takes its correct place. We still have our memories, the skills we learned, our personal likes and dislikes. As a matter of fact, the false self actually becomes better at what it's intended to do, but this conditioned self with all of its past conflict is no longer an intimate enemy. It has been turned to its proper use. It no longer rules us; rather, it is used by something Real within us. The servants no longer run the castle. A state of true higher consciousness is in control, and It meets the world, knowing nothing can take its elevated place except for yet something higher.

You will experience all of this yourself one day if you pursue this great inner work. Reality awaits any individual who puts in the effort to see that the intimate enemy that seemed so foreboding never had any real existence. There really never was a battle to fight, but only something to see. Guy summarized this so clearly as follows. Read it as many times as it takes to allow its message of total self-triumph to speed you on your way to winning the war over the intimate enemy:

> The real struggle in our search for self-victory is to change the nature of our struggle. A whole new kind of action is called for: We must cease our struggles to be victorious over our perceived enemy—and struggle instead to ally ourselves with that which has already won the battle.

Special Summary

. . . Dare to walk away from all of the familiar but useless mental and emotional relationships that give you a temporary but unsatisfactory self. Your true identity is calling to you. But to hear it you must be willing to endure, for as long as necessary, the fear of self-uncertainty. This form of seeming self-abandonment eventually turns into your greatest pleasure as it becomes increasingly evident that the only thing certain about fear is that it will always compromise you. When it comes to who you really are, there is no compromise.

Here is a great mystery. Only when you know who you are not will you know who you really are. Listen for the call of your Royal Nature. Don't be afraid of open spaces. Seek the Truth, not security. You too will make it all the way home to your True Self.

— Guy Finley
The Secret of Letting Go

10

> *This is the greatest stumbling block in our spiritual discipline, which, in actuality, consists not in getting rid of the self but in realizing the fact that there is no such existence from the first.*

— Thomas Merton

POWERFUL ANSWERS TO HELP YOU HELP YOURSELF

Guy receives many letters from grateful readers who are looking for a deeper understanding of their lives through higher principles such as those presented in this book. To help shed additional light on the unique insights into the intimate enemy, and to better assist the reader in his or her efforts to implement the suggested inner work, this last chapter presents a number of Guy's written responses to these ongoing student inquiries.

As you'll read, the content of his individual comments ranges from being very broad in scope to very specific, very personal. In all cases, they are enlightening and encouraging. These letters have been organized to help support and summarize the chapter they best exemplify. To refresh the reader, a brief summary of each chapter is also provided at the beginning of each letter section.

A Brief Note about This Chapter
from Guy Finley

One of the most surprising findings along the upward path to self-victory is that you are not nearly as alone in your struggles or suffering as certain parts of you would have you believe.

The empowering aspect of discovering this widespread general powerlessness among everyone around you is that you start seeing how what you always had taken as just being "your" problem isn't really "yours" at all—in the sense of being personal—but that it belongs to a level of self infused in everyone living from that same unenlightened nature.

This knowledge alone, once grasped even in a small way, diffuses the darkness once believed to be only in your soul. But with this dawning light of Reality comes another benefit that this last chapter in summary will reveal to you.

Since our pains and problems are not really unique, other than the particular form they assume because of our individual life circumstances, this also means that the basic questions we have about how to resolve these conflicts are pretty much in common to all of us.

Allow the following question and answer section to prove to you that you are not alone—either in the sense of being the "only one" who feels the way you do, or in the right sensing that there is, indeed, a way to win for yourself the New Life your Heart of hearts knows you should be living.

———————————————————————— Summary of Chapter One

Unhappy men and women fight to create a place for themselves in, and protect themselves from, what they perceive as a hostile world. However, regardless of what our thoughts tell us, the enemy is not outside of us. The enemy is within us: our mechanical, unconscious reactions that create a threatening world through their own misperceptions. This collection of conditioned mechanical reactions and the host of false self-images it perpetuates is the "intimate enemy." The solution to our problems does not lie in "fixing" what we perceive as the problem "out there." Instead, we must learn to recognize, and drop, the mechanical reactions "in here"; in that level of self that creates the problems in the first place. As we learn how to learn about ourselves, we also increase our power to choose the way of light and consciousness. This is the inner victory that brings all battles to an end.

Question: I've been studying these ideas for some time now, and although I've seen some improvements, I'm still me. I still get disappointed. I still get fooled by others. People do nothing but betray you, and I'm just not strong enough to handle it. And then, it's not easy facing the fact that I'm not always what I say I am. If only I knew for sure there was a happy ending after all this work.

Response: Dear D. B., We must be thrown back upon ourselves over and over again before we can begin to learn the nature of what is really troubling us, for the problems each of us face are undiscovered internal ones, whether we presently see them that way or not. Since the aches we face have their origin in unawareness, awakening to a new awareness is the only solution. This is why it's so very important to persist with our inner work. Only through conscious persistence

does one finally come upon those spiritual lessons that cannot be learned any other way. And D., these lessons *can* be
learned, and their rewards garnered.

No one ever said the Inner Path was easy. If he did, he
either never walked it, or the Path so described was only a day
dream. Yet, nothing is easier than seeing ourselves as we really
are—once we're tired of pretending. Then, the True Path
stretches out before us, and in the miraculous process of letting
go comes the reception of that New Life we've been longing for
all along. It's a Great Mystery indeed, but again, it can be
solved and the treasure made yours.

Question: When I read your books a part of me senses the truth
in them, but sometimes it just seems so hard. I ask myself,
"Why do I have to see all these negative things about myself?"
It's so humiliating and it hurts! Isn't there an easier way?

Response: Dear M. R., The pain you feel is not what it seems. It
only *appears* to be caused by your studying these new ideas.
Please try to always remember the following: the anguish
you may encounter from self-study or meeting any new idea
is *not* that idea's fault. The pain belongs to—and comes
from—that present level of yourself that resists seeing what
the new lesson is revealing about who you have taken yourself to be. A closer look shows that any anguish about ourselves—over ourselves—proves we've taken the wrong side
in the inner battle. Our suffering does not prove we know
what is true; rather it reveals we understand neither ourselves nor our actual inner situation. Persist!

Question: This decision I'm facing has thrown me into torment. How can you know ahead of time which is the best
way to go? I don't want to make the wrong choice, and my
daughter keeps pressuring me to act. How do I weigh my

options to find the answer? Do I even know what all my options are?

Response: Dear N. N., It is never so much the individual things we elect to do, or not to do, that determine the quality of our lives. Rather, it is that spirit which we embrace from moment to moment that makes us what we are, and that gives us our experience of life. The beauty of this finding frees us to take "conscious risks," because bit by bit we come to the life-liberating realization that at all times the only situations we meet are ourselves.

Summary of Chapter Two

When we sense there must be more to life than fighting one painful situation after another, we invite the Truth that heals. Only when we say honestly, "I don't understand this pain," does Truth have the chance to reveal a new understanding to us that straightens out "the crooked road." Every seemingly painful condition is no more than a temporary conjunction of factors, with our own perception being one of the most important contributing elements. With time, all conditions change. Hence, the wise counsel, "this too shall pass." When we stop valuing the sense of self we derive from our unhappiness, and withdraw our own unconscious contribution to the perpetuation of the difficulty, the problem falls away of itself. Our inward development transforms every outer condition.

Question: I've been trying so hard to "make something of myself," but I keep coming up against a brick wall. Every time I come close to making it, something happens to ruin my plans. I'm beginning to suspect that I'm the one who's doing myself in, but if that's true, I'm at a complete loss. Is it wrong to try to be a success? And why won't I let myself be one?

Response: My Friend R., There really are Answers to our questions; solid, complete answers which can bring an end to
our frustrations. But these answers must come to us from *a
level above the disturbance*. Once this important principle is
grasped, our lives become centered on working on ways to
elevate our understanding; for now we know: the blockages
we encounter—and feel—are reflections of our "present" life
level. Changing, by outgrowing, these levels is the same as
removing their barriers.

Surely you've seen by now that the harder you push to
succeed, the more elusive that success becomes. There are real
reasons for this phenomenon, reasons that, once understood,
not only free us from our former frustrations, but, paradoxi-
cally, deliver to us that which we wanted all along!

Question: I gather from your books that we shouldn't be
caught up in financial worries, but in a practical world, I
don't know how you can avoid it. Recently, I made some
bad business decisions, and now it looks as though I could
lose everything I've taken years to build up. I should have
known better than to make those mistakes. Looking back on
it, I really don't know what came over me. Now, I don't trust
myself to do anything right anymore, and I wonder if I've
ever really known what was right for me or anyone else.

I sense that spiritual ideas hold the answer, but I just
don't see how to apply them to a situation like this. How
can an "idea" help you when you're facing not being able to
take care of yourself and your family at the most elementary
level? I guess I've always thought money and possessions
would keep me safe. Now that I'm losing them, I'm afraid.

Response: Dear J., First, your feelings of vulnerability are signs
that you're starting to wake up just a bit. As a man discovers

more and more of the often humiliating truth about his present level of development, he also realizes he is not in charge
of anything other than the explanations he can create for
himself about his own shortcomings. So, the dawning of the
feeling that you are not able to depend on what you've
always counted on to see you through tough times is a good
sign that promises the possibility of learning to depend on
something beyond what you have always embraced as yourself, something that won't let you down in times of trial.
This is what we are working for!

As far as what to do about those fears of not having
enough, etc., you must take care of your family's *practical*
needs. This is your responsibility, but—on the other hand—
ask yourself the following question: can anything I'm afraid
to live without ever be the source of my fearlessness? The
answer is obviously a resounding No! But what does this
discovery teach us?

What good is anything we may have if all it can do for us
is make us frightened that one day we may not have enough
of "it"—whatever that "it" may be: money, approval, family,
friends, etc. We must get tired of being frightened that one
day we may not have enough of what it is in our lives that
has already proved itself powerless to make us fearless
human beings. *Our problem is fear itself,* and not *the object*
that that fear in us tells us we must possess in order to possess ourselves. Consider this idea and let it show you its
secret strength.

Question: Well, Guy, I'm happy to report that things finally
seem to be working out. All the problems I had at work
have smoothed over, and I've met a woman who really
seems to have her head on straight, but I don't want to slip
into complacency over this. Any advice?

Response: Dear J. P., I'm happy to learn that all is on track for
     you. The two most important times for a man to work
     harder than ever in his inner work is when things seem to
     be going the best they can and when they turn the other
     way. In other words, don't let good fortune—or bad—keep
     you from your inner work. *Everything* in life turns around
     and around. The Truth alone always faces you with a smile.

———————————————— Summary of Chapter Three

Negative states are like hitchhiking spirits that invade our psychic systems without our awareness. Once these foreign forces
have moved in, we accept and unconsciously nurture these
states because they give us a powerful sense of self. Through
our attention, we give them our life force and find reasons to
justify their existence. What we hate and fear is not something
real, but our own thoughts that interpret a situation as being
bad—an enemy that is a creation of our own mind! We can
drop our fascination with these hitchhiking spirits and see
them for the passing states they are. We need not fight them or
give in to them, but only come awake and go silent in their
presence. In this way, we deny them our life energy and are no
longer surrounded by enemies that we ourselves created.

Question: [Letter begins with an account of how the writer lost
     money in a business deal after being tricked by two men.]
     I'm ashamed to admit it, but I'm angry and resentful—two
     emotions I'd thought I'd gotten well past. It's still hard to
     believe I could have fallen for such an obvious scam, and
     that two men I thought were my friends could have stolen
     from me what I had hoped to be my children's legacy. I'm
     burning up inside with rage, and guilt, and concern over
     what my children will do now. I know this is killing me.
     What would you do in my position?

Response: Dear Dr. H., There are no words of philosophy that can comfort you in these times of personal trial as outlined in your letter to me, so I will not offer any. You did ask, however, how I would "handle" the situation were I in your shoes. To begin with, I would muster everything I could find in me and, whatever the personal cost, I would refuse to be self-pitying.

Then, I would start over, right from the beginning, whatever that may be—or wherever that may take me. There is no power on earth that can interfere with this intention and act.

Next, instead of falling into despair over my losses, I would deeply examine what it is inside of me that feels all I am worth is money, or whatever it says to me I've lost, and then I would get busy losing interest in that nature that calls itself by my name.

Hatred of anyone, or anything, destroys the one who hates. This is unequivocal spiritual law—so I would do all that I could to lay down my resentments by seeing that all I'm doing is burning myself up with wasted energies that could be put to productive purposes.

Lastly, I would seriously consider, not what it is that I think I won't be able to leave my children, but what it is that I'm giving them with my current attitudes and example. Then, as tough as it may be to act it out, I would make it abundantly clear to them through my revised actions that a man is not what he possesses, but is, rather, what possesses him. And since it's possible to choose what possesses you, which you start doing by refusing to be possessed of dark spirits, this means you can choose in favor—over and over again as many times as necessary—of what's authentically good and true for you.

Question: It seems that every time I get close to making a
breakthrough, some negative emotion takes me over and I
feel weaker, and less able to handle anything than ever. For
example, I actually had a few days of feeling good, and then
this depression came over me that held me for days. I could
not work on myself, or even pick up a book the whole time.
It makes me wonder whether there's any hope for me, and if
it would be better not to pursue changing myself at all.

Response: Dear S. S., Let me begin by telling you that just as
there are Favorable Forces working to help us win our Spiritual Freedom, so too are there those forces which exist
solely to prevent this inner success. Those lower forces must
try and block our way out because as we find it, these anti-
spiritual powers die accordingly.

So, have no concern—or as little as possible anyway—for
what stands in your way. I know this isn't easy to do, but
keep your eye on what you know to be true, instead of letting it be directed by fearful forces to gaze upon what they
want you to see. The mounting negativity we feel as we
progress along the path is darkness' heightened effort to
turn us away. I know this to be true. And so will you if you
just persist. Nothing real can stand in our way, and everything that is Real wants us to succeed.

Always try to remember the following: all negative feelings are just illusions of power, not real powers in and of
themselves. But, the only way to learn this secret, this truth
which frees us, is to challenge these states with our new and
higher understanding of their true nature.

Question: My little boy is driving me up the wall! I just can't
control him. I try to be loving with him, like the experts say,
but I can only put up with him for so long. Then he does

something that goes beyond even my patience, and I lash out, which of course is followed by great guilt. His teachers at school keep sending me letters telling me what a problem he is, but it seems that whatever they do with him makes him worse. They let him get away with anything as long as he doesn't physically harm another child, and by the end of a week of school he's completely out of control. I've been reading books on the subject, but one tells you to be permissive (which I know doesn't work) and one tells you to be strict (which makes me feel guilty). I'm at my wits' end. Is there any real answer to all of this?

Response: Dear D. F., The real answer to your question is that we can never give anyone anything that we ourselves don't possess.

Most so-called teachers approach these problems with behavior in the same way they've dealt with their own neurotic behavior—which is to say, they don't have a clue what to do about negative states. So, not knowing how to treat themselves, other than knowing they hated how they were treated when they were growing up, the only approach they can offer is the opposite one to the one that didn't work on them. No opposite can clear up the condition its opposite calls into existence.

All children must be disciplined, but this doesn't mean punished by the supervising adult's own negative states. There is such a thing as kind strictness, strong correction, unyielding direction. We don't treat kids right, so that they grow and learn right values, because when the time comes for us to be the right person, there's residual wrongness in us: anger, fear, resentment. You know the story. Rather than facing our own weaknesses, we accept the child's and hope they will turn out right, because we say that we're doing the "loving" thing by letting them find their own way. Don't mistake what I'm saying. It's necessary to accept a child's shortcomings, but that child must not be allowed to start accepting his or her negative states or acts as necessary. And what else can they do if that's what you or I do with them?

Summary of Chapter Four

People are not the singular selves they appear to be, but are secretly a multiplicity. As we unconsciously identify ourselves with each different "I" that takes the stage we mistakenly believe that it is who we are, but each of these selves is just a creation of a temporary conjunction of conditions. These changing selves, or false senses of "I," arise continually out of our conditioned false nature. Each momentary "I" is called the Temporary Person in Charge, or TPIC. TPICs pop out to deal with situations the false nature "sees," but these "situations" we struggle with are really nothing other than an interpretation of life—itself being the result of our conditioned response to events. A TPIC has no staying power. It changes as the conjunction of conditions in life changes. Our observation of this fact is key to changing our relationship with the false self. As our growing awareness of the TPICs causes their power to fade, something real and permanent begins to reveal itself from within.

Question: I was hoping things would get easier for me as I got older, but it seems every day I'm faced with problems at my business, and people are always making demands of me, and I just don't know when to do what. The more I do to try to settle things, the more entangled they get. Nothing ever gets resolved. All that happens is that one problem just fades away, and then a new problem comes up. I always saw myself as a problem-solver, but now I'm beginning to suspect that I'm the problem!

Response: Dear E. R., That we "don't know when to do what" isn't the problem. Where we're all tied up is that we really don't know what we tell ourselves that we do! This is the fundamental problem, and it's a spiritual one that can only be resolved through spiritual self-discovery, discoveries that finally lead us to see that since we aren't who we've always "thought" ourselves to be, then neither are our "problems" (which arise in thought) what we perceive them to be. I know this isn't easy, but better than which side to choose in a fight is living where there are no fights, no conflict at all. Then you've won. Completely.

Real spiritual discovery requires what has to feel like a risk to our false nature. We're ultimately called to see that our thinking—what we "think" we know—is the source of our confusion, and not the way out of it. As this becomes inwardly clear, then and only then does thought—and all of its nagging questions—take its proper place in our lives and become our servant, instead of us, its.

Question: I'm determined to do what you say and "wake up." So far, though, nothing significant has happened. Am I doing something wrong?

Response: Dear R. A., The essence of making real spiritual discoveries, and winning the peace that attends those insights, hinges upon a man realizing what is within his power, and what's not. The everyday mind is not meant or empowered to create the higher well-being he seeks, and this is where it seems to get foggy for most. When his mind realizes what it can and can't do, then it begins to let go. As it negates its own activity, born from this new understanding of what it actually is, it quiets down, a man begins to wake up to reality and in flows something unthinkable! Keep going! There is a way out.

Question: I've always tried to play by the rules, but the rules
keep changing. For years I devoted myself to my career; and
my family suffered. Then I got a new family. But now my
energies are so divided, I can't do anything the way it should
be done. Nothing has given me what I thought it would. I'm
no closer to feeling in control of my life than I did when I
was 16. Now I'm trying this "spiritual path," and it's thrown
me into conflict about all the other aspects of my life. Everything I do is to reach some kind of "promised land," but the
more I do, the further away from ever reaching it I feel. I'm
beginning to doubt that I'll ever know the right way to go.

Response: Dear P. V., Your question to me, which I'll rephrase,
is one every sincere seeker must eventually put to herself if
she is to succeed in her own Liberation: "Why do I keep
running to find a place to Rest?"

The very fact that this question occurs to anyone is rare,
and even less likely is that the mind which first wonders
about "why" it's doing what it's doing will ever really consider the implications of its own intuition. In fact, the clearer
this obvious contradiction in your mind becomes, the more
frightened that mind (false nature) will become, which
means many, many things, all of which are valuable points
of study. For instance, the axiom "a house divided cannot
stand" implies in this circumstance that your new awareness
that you may be "spinning your wheels" with your present
way of seeking can't be coming to you from the same nature
as the one that has you out "racing to find rest." Why?
Because the false nature wants its vain and self glorifying
dreams to go on and on. Of course, this idiot nature is completely oblivious to the fact it not only has no future, but it
has no Real Presence either.

I've found, as a good rule of thumb, that whenever it
seems as though there's been a dawning of a sort, especially

if that insight is frightening to the "known structure of self," then that flash is usually some form of real Light, some Real Insight. The fear that follows, those inner voices which slowly undermine what's been exposed with a barrage of intellectualized reasons are just the old, mechanical, self-loving nature wanting to keep things in the dark—and keep you there with it as well. Let the Truth lead. And one way to follow the dawning light is to keep turning your back on the darkness.

Question: My problem is letting go. I'm always offering myself solutions, and I don't know how to stop. They make so much sense at the time, but then I end up in more trouble than before.

Response: Dear M. M., The problem is the tenacious nature of thought. It's forever reproducing itself, reincarnating as it were, its temporary life. Thought floats within reach of thought packed together in communities of association like housing projects upon cluttered hillsides—where the neighbors clamor and conflict breeds, but from which no one moves away for fear of losing the security of false familiarity. This is why we must develop the natural distaste for our own thought-life, for this creates natural discernment leading to detachment, to letting go.

Question: I don't trust myself anymore. I'm afraid to make any move at all. I thought that if I tried to find God my life would start to make more sense to me—not less! Have I taken a wrong turn somewhere?

Response: Dear A. C., Virtually no one understands that before the coming of the Light there must come what is perceived to be (by the false nature) the onset of darkness. This is a stage that cannot be avoided, must not be feared, and that, if entered into willingly, will eventually show itself not to be the darkness at all! This is the Great Mystery which only the Conscious Journey can "solve." Give your heart to the Truth. It knows exactly what to do with it. As this much gets clearer to you, starts the most wonderful adventure this world can offer anyone.

— Summary of Chapter Five

We suffer over conditions that seem more powerful than we are, but, in fact, it is the TPIC's view that makes the situation painful. A new view of any contrary condition transforms it into something completely different. As we've seen throughout history, people who learn to look at life for its hidden lesson always seem to rise above adversity to find lives of Higher meaning. The first step is to learn to doubt our suffering. For example, we suffer because so many things in life seem impermanent. When we see that our hope for these things to provide us with permanence has been misplaced all along, we can find something beyond our own plans that is truly permanent. As a second example, we suffer over the burden of self-imposed responsibility, thinking we can and must control the events of life. This suffering disappears when we realize we are not responsible to control life, but only to allow our awakened awareness to understand life.

Question: I long for the truth to take over my life. I love reading your books because they make me feel it's possible. They spark something in me, but then it goes away. I can't seem to take any of the good feeling with me when I go out in the world. I still suffer all the old feelings of disappointment and resentment. A whole day goes by without once thinking about the truth because I'm so caught up in worries. It makes me wonder if what you say will ever take hold. Sometimes I feel like "damp wood." No matter what I do, I'll never catch fire.

Response: Dear C. R., Our present nature is happy being discontented. Now I know this sounds like a strange, impossible situation, but nevertheless, it's true. This ceaseless season of discontent provides it (us) with virtually an endless road to walk down in our thoughts, and eventual actions. Of course, as you've seen, this road goes nowhere at all, but here's the point as it applies to your question.

This false self has its own nature, its own "unlife," and it's not about to welcome the Light or actions which will show it to be only a shadow, an imitation of life. While it's true that it feels like we're damp wood, it's also true that beneath the years of soaked-in lies about the real nature of life, there lies the "good wood," which, if submitted persistently to the light of new and higher insight, will dry out and ignite! Then the process starts over again at a new and deeper level within. This is why you must persist!

Question: Why do people have to be so cruel to each other? I can't begin to tell you the shock and disappointment I feel over these events [which are described in detail earlier in the letter]. I just can't understand why it has to be this way. Is there no such thing as loyalty or decency anymore? Why are so many people only "in it for themselves." Is there any hope for people?

Response: Hello D., As sorry as it may seem, your tale of betrayal and defeat is not uncommon at all. You would be stunned, and hopefully one day you will be, at just how sad the human condition remains, unnecessarily so. In a world where all its people know is secret fear, it's no wonder everyone acts out their lives in secret conspiracies and twisted plots—all designed to bring about a security which is destroyed (from within) the moment they begin to conspire. But here's the real answer for those of us who want a Higher Life. Leave the dead to bury the dead. We have, as I know you're beginning to understand, more important work to be about.

Question: I'm very bitter over the fact that my husband won't give up his drinking to save our marriage. It's been six months since I threatened to move out, but I can't seem to do it. I'm so angry at him for doing this to me and making me feel this way. If only he'd try. Life wasn't supposed to be this way. I wanted the vine-covered cottage, but the reality turned out to be quite different. I wish the problem would just disappear, and I also know what a waste of time it is to think that way. If only I could get over hoping things would work out, maybe I could move on with my life.

Response: Dear C. M., One of the biggest problems we all have, that seems to be connected to the behavior of others, really has nothing to do at all with them. We tend to look in the wrong places for the love we sense should be in our lives. When people betray us, the great pain we experience hasn't so much to do with their transgression as it does with what the blow their act does to our hopes for real love. The pain of our disappointment, grief, and so on is mostly that of realizing we've once again been looking for something permanent in the temporary.

Going through these upheavals, and the discoveries they lead to, does not mean you give up on someone you love, but we must learn to let what life is trying to teach us do just that. Not wanting the lesson doesn't make it go away. All that happens is the pain of it grows worse, and worse, until we really blow up and walk away from the situation, only to find out we've really changed nothing, because all along, the problem was in our level of spiritual understanding. The hardest thing to do in any troubling time is to ask Truth to show you what you need to see about you. But do it anyway!

_____ Summary of Chapter Six

Inner development requires work and a willingness to learn from experience. We prevent this life-healing process when we become defensive and refuse to admit our error. We begin to change when we stop blaming reality, accept that it was our lack of understanding that created the problem, and learn the lesson for next time. For example, like the little boy who faced the "haunted house," our self-investigation shows us it is not necessary to fear anything within us. We need not go along with any TPIC's negative interpretation. In the past, we've always jumped on one wild emotional carriage after another and been carried off. But we can learn to change this self-betraying behavior by taking a "psychic pause." Even if we wake up to ourselves after we've already been taken over by a wild emotion, we need not fight the state. We need only become aware. When we win the inner victory, no state or condition can conquer us again.

Question: I must have a really hard head! For forty-three years I've been chasing one dream after another. I keep looking at other people and thinking they have something I don't. Then, I go after what they have, thinking this time it's got to work. No matter how many times I am disappointed, I'm ready to go after the next thing. Am I ever going to learn to stop running? Even though I feel that what you say is right, and I have to give up looking for the answer this way, I still feel pulled. Surely, somebody out there must be happy.

There must be something I can do to get the brass ring. What am I not seeing?

Response: Dear K. R., As Shakespeare wrote, "all the world is a stage and all are actors upon it." The problem is that no one knows they're acting! No one sees the discrepancy between the happiness they profess before others (and to themselves in the dimly lit theater of their own mental movies), and the suffering they actually experience.

This is why the human condition is beyond description, so badly degenerated, spiritually speaking. But, in that great spiritual paradox called higher consciousness or rebirth, it's in one's personal discovery of this lost, sleeping condition of ours that we actually begin to wake up from it, and awakening from the dream of unhappiness must begin by disturbing the dreamer. Ask Truth to help you wake up!

Question: First of all, I want to thank you. You've really made me see certain mistakes I've been making, and I've been working hard with these ideas. But I'm not strong enough yet, and now that I'm going through this awful divorce, I can't seem to control my reactions at all. I want to be true to the noble way of life you describe in your books, but then I find myself acting like an idiot. With the trial coming up, I'm afraid something will be let loose in me that I really don't want to see. My husband knows how to push every one of my buttons, and I don't think it would be right to let him get away with what he's trying to do. How can I be true to the higher, when everything low in me is screaming for revenge?

Response: Dear D. L., Nothing makes me happier than to hear of someone who, in finding the truth, knows that she has also begun to find herself. This is what all of us are here for:

to rediscover, as it were, our True, Original Life—the One which has its beginning in Spirit. But, having "found" this new direction, and walking in it, are two different orders of our existence—as your letter tells me you are in the process of finding out. The question of how we stay true to this higher life in the face of those events that seem mean and low is a natural one, but unfortunately, the answer has to be reached through trial by fire—and I'm not referring to what awaits you in court!

The trial by fire, regardless of appearances, is always the same one. The only thing that ever troubles us in this life is the demands we've placed upon it. I will offer you a lesson in the form of two questions I recommend you put to yourself daily.

First, does it make any sense to light myself on fire because someone else, anyone else, insists on burning—for whatever reason? Second, if someone else is on fire, already burning with mental and emotional flames, what need do I have to punish that person further, or to show that person the error of his or her ways, especially when all he or she wants to do is burn? D., be as True as you know how, do what's right without burning, and get on with your real life. You can't have what's new and cling to the old.

Letting go of ourselves is the trial by fire, the den of lions. We must do what's true even when we are sure it spells the end for who we've always been. Do it! You'll get the help you need to succeed. This is truth's Promise.

Question: Some problems just seem too hard to handle just by trying to respond differently. What do you do when somebody else is doing everything possible to make your life miserable? I love my wife, and I believe she loves me, but she can be so cruel and cutting at times. She knows just how to hurt me, and no matter what I do to change myself, she's going to continue to do it. How will watching myself change her?

Response: Dear J. W., We are only in wrong relationship with others to the degree that we are trying to take something from that relationship. Your wife is not the problem, although abusive people punish everyone, including themselves. As long as you find her to be the reason why you are experiencing life the way in which you've described, your situation will not, cannot, change.

There is nothing as important as your wish for a new, fully free life. Refuse to accept anything less and you can be certain that whatever questions may arise from your spiritual work, they will be answered by the same Spirit which has led you up to that point. So, persist with your spiritual studies. You'll soon see, increasingly, that the whole world changes for you in direct proportion to your new realization about what this world is for: namely, your deliberate inner development. As you grow you'll realize something that cannot be understood until then: desert winds neither move nor disturb mountain pines.

Summary of Chapter Seven

It is possible to find that right authority within that can prevail over all the touchy, demanding TPICs and their constant battling with reality. Two especially powerful methods can help us. The first method tells us to become aware that life on the battlefield makes no sense, and then put in for an inner transfer. This special kind of spiritual transfer involves turning the whole thing over to something higher, and we will when we see the futility in believing we can win ultimate victory on the battlefield. The second method shows us how, like Michael the

Mighty Ram, to find our own inner place of safety that protects us from all conditions. Key to this process is developing a single-minded, clear purpose for ourselves, so that finding this true, higher life becomes more valuable to us than any temporary victory on the battlefield.

Question: When I look at myself, it seems that my most prevalent emotion is anger. It's always there. I frequently find myself caught up in what you call "mental movies," remembering all the cruelty and unfairness. I know that indulging in this does no good, but I feel powerless to stop these raging thoughts. What can I do? I really am weary of my own out-of-control emotions.

Response: Dear G. C., You already know, I could infer from your letter, that your anger is destroying you. It is—and it will. You also know, to your spiritual credit, that there is no justification for the endless self-defeat which giving yourself over to hostile feelings entails. The fact that you are tired of losing your life to these self-harming psychic states means you are ready for a change. Here is a new way to work with what's been working you over.

The next time some hostile state takes you over, either in thought—as in remembering something someone did to you in the past—or in an actual moment of conflict with someone standing before you, take the following inner steps as soon as you can remember yourself to do so. Start by seeing that something foreign to your True Nature has imposed itself on you, taken over your life. Once having done this, do nothing else except realize that while you may be temporarily powerless to stop the lower state from possessing you, you are empowered to recognize the negative state as the intruder that it is. This awareness, this conscious, unselfjustifying awareness of your true pained condition, is what it means to put the Light on the problem. That's your job. The Light will do its part if you'll do yours. Persist until you are free!

Question: Your teachings say that making demands and having expectations just sets us up for trouble. I know it's true. I always plan how other people should act and how things should turn out, but they never do what I expect, and then I become angry and disappointed. I sense that I am causing all my own pain. If I could just learn to want for myself what life wants for me maybe I wouldn't be afraid anymore. But I can't imagine how to even start letting go in this way. How do I let go of my own thoughts? How do I learn to see things in a new way?

Response: Dear R. U., Let's just say that freedom from anger, disappointments, and frustration comes in direct proportion to our realization that looking to any fearful thought or feeling for guidance, or a sense of self, is like asking a ghost to show you the way out of a haunted house. Which brings us face to face with the most difficult question of all: if I don't interact with my habitual thoughts and feelings, if I don't find a direction from their influences, then how and from where will I know to take my "next" step?

Letting go is about learning to die to ourselves, psychologically, so that something Higher, something "Undiminishable" can stand in for us. This switch takes place as we learn to stand down consciously. This new action can be done, but it takes both insight and being sick and tired of being angry and tense. Our inner studies prepare us for what we need to see about ourselves to set us on the path to freedom from all frustrations.

Question: You write about living in the "now," and say we
   should try to stay always in the present moment. I do try to
   remember myself, but it's a constant struggle. I look for a
   place of peace, but never find it. If anything, my own mind
   seems to do everything it can to distract me. Why do I keep
   fighting what I really want?

Response: Hello V., Yes, it's true. The ideal would be to live
   firmly spiritually seated in the perfectly present moment.
   This time we call *now* isn't really a time at all, but is a timeless, eternal, and everlastingly new kingdom. It resides
   within us, really, where our real life does, even though we
   presently perceive our lives as being outside of us. Our
   awareness of the present moment *is* this present moment,
   which is why remaining inwardly awake is the same as
   anchoring ourselves in the perfectly present moment. So,
   persist! That which pulls us from the present moment is our
   false, time nature. As we learn to see through its thought
   life, and let it go, in floods what is permanent and lastingly
   peaceable.

_____ Summary of Chapter Eight

What we find in life is based on where we put our attention.
When we focus on the small worlds our thoughts create, we
miss out on the beauty and possibilities we are meant to enjoy.
The way to life liberation is summarized in the timeless phrase,
"Know Thyself." Through self-study we see through the
thought self and its fleeting TPICs, and ultimately find something true and permanent. Self-study requires complete honesty. We must not imagine ourselves as we hope to be. Rather,
we must see that we are not what our self-images tell us. If we
let self-study show us what is true, it will take us to a higher life

beyond anything we can presently imagine. The encouraging fact is that however many times we may fail, we can always begin anew. And indeed, when higher self-knowledge is our only aim, there can never be failure, but only new steps on our road to final victory.

Question: As I walk the spiritual path, I always come to a new bend in the road. I think I'm getting a handle on myself, and then I realize I don't know myself at all. Do things ever get clearer?

Response: Dear D. C., Working with truthful principles always produces a kind of special turning point for us over and over again, one which presents the possibility of not only a New Direction in life, but all of the new adventures—disappointments and discoveries that this New and Higher Road promises. We must persist, for there is always something higher than what we perceive in our present view. So, this is what I say to you. Persist. The True, New Life awaits anyone who wants the True, New Life!

Question: I need some encouragement. "Working on myself" seems to have no end, and I don't know what to make of myself anymore. I look at my friends who don't know anything about this, and they never seem to question themselves. I'm not saying they're happy, but at least they're not always second-guessing themselves. I know you're right about there being something better in life we can reach for, but when do we begin to see things getting better?

Response: Dear A. P., Be assured there are real solutions, and that with patient inner work, you will know them, and their peace, which brings us to your conflict about the Path and your difficulties.

A., imagine a person climbing a hill in order to reach the other side where there is a beautiful view. His or her perspective of the climb, especially as the top is approached, is that it's arduous, a painful ordeal. But now imagine someone who has reached the other side and is walking down its gentle slope, enjoying the whole affair. This person's perspective is that the climb was worth the price paid. So, do you see? Yes, the inner work is difficult, in some stages, but in other stages, that work is worth 1,000 times the effort. And best of all, these kinds of spiritual rewards never fade away as do our Earthly ones.

Question: It's probably just an excuse, but I often feel that if my circumstances were different, I'd be making better progress in my spiritual life. I'm so caught up in responsibilities to my family and my job, and my own drive to achieve, that I keep getting pulled away from what I know I should do. My wife doesn't make it any easier. I try to talk to her about higher principles, but she just doesn't get it. I think I'm approaching my inner work with the same over-achiever in me that makes all my external activities such a problem. I can't give up in either place. Am I going to have to make a choice between being a success and waking up? And how do I make that choice?

Response: Dear J.C., You must make a living. Where's the problem in that? Each day apply yourself to the degree needed to supply your householder requirements. Take care of your wife. Don't expect her to understand what you don't; but if you work hard to become a spiritual man, she'll see this, be attracted to your inner life, and she'll follow you to the ends of the Earth.

Stop struggling to find what you think are those peaceful feelings. Real inner quiet is first an understanding. The higher feelings follow naturally, without any concern or effort.

The Truth knows what's in a man's heart. So, his job is to find out what the Truth already knows. Discovering himself is his part of the arrangement, and this he can do anywhere, under any circumstances. Believe me. Ask the Truth to show you what you need to see and then keep your eyes open when reality appears. Everything else is then done for you.

———————————————— Summary of Chapter Nine

Our pain reflects the fact that we feel cut off. We blame external conditions, but there is really only one reason: as each TPIC turns in upon itself to make itself feel complete, it cuts us off from reality. By imposing itself and its distorted interpretation between what is our True Nature and the world, this false nature—the intimate enemy—cuts us off from true understanding and right action. When we can catch any TPIC in the act of "turning in," we free ourselves of its false authority. Then we can experience life in the first person, and every moment becomes the original moment it is created to be. By "opening the circle," the lines of energy are reestablished between the individual and Truth or God. The false nature no longer distorts life by trying to be the ruling being, and instead takes its rightful place as a servant to the True Self. It is no longer an intimate enemy, and the war within has been won.

Question: My time is spent between a rock and a hard place. I'm always frustrated when things don't go correctly, and I'm unable to control anything the way I know I should. I find your approach very tempting as an end to all these difficulties. However, I hesitate to really embark on the path you set forth, because although I would like the peace it promises, I'm afraid that if I just let go, things will fall apart. If I empty my mind of my thoughts, who will take care of things? I have no idea what it means to live my life without me being in charge.

Response: Dear K. H., Working to see into and to quiet the mind does not mean you are "running on empty," walking around vacant. In fact, the whole process of freeing the mind from its own content has nothing to do with those aspects of practical thought with which we need to drive a car, read a book, or cook a meal. In many ways, the "emptying" of the mind isn't something we "do" at all. Freedom comes to our inner life, emotional and mental, as we recognize that there are those parts of ourselves that can *serve* — and then there are parts that *steal*.

We learn to live with and guide the parts that serve us. These "parts" include the thoughts and feelings that help us to get around, that remember necessary details, that can be inspired and impassioned. These aspects of our psyche are beneficial and necessary to our physical existence. But they are—or at least they're intended to be—servants of both our practical life as well as our higher mental and emotional needs.

On the other hand, there are those aspects of our nature that don't serve our being, but steal it. These seemingly self-serving thoughts and feelings are what we experience in our psychic system as negatives, as conflict-producing mental and emotional activities. It's the level of the student's spiritual development which determines his or her sensitivity to these intruders and their covert thievery, but here's the point: as we awaken to these sensation-producing, but life-stealing inner entities, we realize their existence within us

has been by unconscious consent. Actually, to be more accurate, the mind itself "wakes up" to the contradictions within
itself. As it does, it naturally lets go of the processes which it
had been either creating or permitting to go on unrestricted.
This is what "emptying" the mind is; otherwise, the actions
we take to free ourselves are only secret ways in which we
further bind ourselves up by adding yet another notion—
one more incomplete idea to ourselves—about the real
nature of Freedom.

Question: You say that every prayer is answered, but in my
own experience, I've been praying for help, and have
received none. Part of the problem is I don't even know
what kind of help I want. How can I ask for something I
myself don't understand?

Response: Dear C. M., I know it seems difficult to understand
sometimes, but the Truth works in strange ways. We often
find what we're really looking for when we least expect to
find it . . . or when we've just given up hope of ever finding
anything at all. That's why we must persist. We must keep
our wish alive to be a different, Higher kind of individual.
The Universe hears our silent, heartfelt wishes to be new, to
know something higher, and if we'll be true to that wish, the
Truth will find a way to grant it.

Question: I often try during the day to start over, but quite
honestly, no matter what I tell myself, I rarely feel anything
dramatic happening. I may become aware of myself for a
moment, but I can't seem to get free of my anger, or nervousness, or whatever else I'm feeling at the time. Maybe I'm
trying too hard, but it seems that nothing new ever happens.

Response: Dear L. T., To really "start over" is not a mental
process, although the mind must be used for the approach—

much as a ladder leads up to a wall—but can't take you over to the other side—a leap is needed.

Your Real Nature, call it what you will, is a present being. This elevated Self does not need to start over because it dwells permanently in the now. These aren't just words. There really does exist this nature, as well as the possibility of our dwelling within its ever-present life. Defeat and its myriad problems don't exist for this Self, because it has no past. It's new now. And so can we be new now, if we're first fed up inwardly with our old, false nature; and secondly if we're willing to really let go of this nature as we understand what that means. That's what our higher studies are for: to grow in greater and greater understanding that leads up to a whole new and now nature.

In short, we need to wake up. You can do it right now. Put this letter down and just be quietly aware of yourself— without thinking about it. This kind of awareness suspends habitual, self-referencing thought, and in that momentary absence of the mechanical thought nature, we touch another life: one whose nature is the same as "starting over."

Special Summary

It is not the condition we find ourselves in that determines the work we can do to free ourselves. This is what the false self wants us to believe. Just the opposite is true. It is work we do on ourselves that actually changes the conditions we are in, whatever they may be.

— Guy Finley
The Secret of Letting Go

Stay in Touch . . .

Llewellyn publishes hundreds of books on your favorite subjects. On the following pages you will find listed some books now available on related subjects. Your local bookstore stocks most of these and will stock new Llewellyn titles as they become available. We urge your patronage.

Order by Phone

Call toll-free within the U.S. and Canada, 1-800-THE MOON.
In Minnesota call (612) 291-1970.
We accept Visa, MasterCard, and American Express.

Order by Mail

Send the full price of your order (MN residents add 7% sales tax) in U.S. funds to:

> Llewellyn Worldwide
> P.O. Box 64383, Dept. K697-1
> St. Paul, MN 55164-0383, U.S.A.

Postage and Handling

The following charges are valid for the U.S., Mexico, and Canada only:

- ◆ $4.00 for orders $15.00 and under
- ◆ $5.00 for orders over $15.00
- ◆ No charge for orders over $100.00

We ship UPS in the continental United States. We ship to P.O. boxes via standard mail only. Orders shipped to Alaska, Hawaii, Virgin Islands, and Puerto Rico will be sent first-class mail. Orders shipped to Mexico and Canada are shipped via surface mail only.
International orders: Airmail—add freight equal to price of each book to the total price of order, plus $5.00 for each non-book item (audiotapes, etc.). Surface mail—add $1.00 per item.
Allow 4–6 weeks delivery on all orders. Postage and handling rates subject to change.

Group Discounts

We offer a 20% quantity discount to group leaders or agents. You must order a minimum of 5 copies of the same book to get our special quantity price.

Free Catalog

Get a free copy of our color catalog, *New Worlds of Mind and Spirit*. Subscribe for just $10.00 in the United States and Canada ($30.00 overseas, airmail). Many bookstores carry *New Worlds*—ask for it!

Freedom from the Ties that Bind

Guy Finley

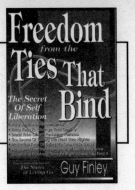

Imagine how your life would flow *without* the weight of those weary inner voices constantly convincing you that "you can't," or complaining that someone else should be blamed for the way *you* feel. The weight of the world on your shoulders would be replaced by a bright, new sense of freedom. Fresh, new energies would flow. *You could choose to live the way* YOU *want.* In *Freedom from the Ties that Bind,* Guy Finley reveals hundreds of Celestial, but down-to-earth, secrets of Self-Liberation that show you exactly how to be fully independent, and *free of any condition not to your liking.* Even the most difficult people won't be able to turn your head or test your temper. Enjoy solid, meaningful relationships founded *in conscious choice*—not *through self-defeating compromise.* Learn the secrets of unlocking the door to your own Free Mind. Be empowered to break free of any self-punishing pattern, and make the discovery that who you really are is already everything you've ever wanted to be.

0-87542-217-9
240 pp., 6 x 9, softcover $10.00

The Secret of
Letting Go

Guy Finley

Whether you need to let go of a
painful heartache, a destructive
habit, a frightening worry or a
nagging discontent, *The Secret of Letting Go* shows you
how to call on your own hidden powers and how they
can take you through and beyond any challenge or problem. This book reveals the secret source of a brand-new
kind of inner strength.

In the light of your new and higher self-understanding,
emotional difficulties such as loneliness, fear, anxiety and
frustration fade into nothingness as you happily discover
they never really existed in the first place.

With a foreword by Desi Arnaz Jr., and introduction by
Dr. Jesse Freeland, *The Secret of Letting Go* is a pleasing
balance of questions and answers, illustrative examples,
truth tales, and stimulating dialogues that allow the
reader to share in the exciting discoveries that lead up to
lasting self-liberation.

This is a book for the discriminating, intelligent, and sen-
sitive reader who is looking for *real* answers.

0-87542-223-3
240 pp., 5¼ x 8, softcover $9.95

The Secret Way of Wonder

Guy Finley

The Secret Way of Wonder

WONDER

Insights from the Silence

Guy Finley
author of *The Secret of Letting Go*
Introduction by Desi Arnaz, Jr.
Foreword by Dr. Ellen Dickstein
Special Message from Vernon Howard

Discover an inner world of wisdom and make miracles happen! Here is a simple yet deeply effective system of illuminating and eliminating the problems of inner mental and emotional life.

The Secret Way of Wonder is an interactive spiritual workbook offering guided practice for self-study. It is about Awakening the Power of Wonder in yourself. A series of 60 "Wonders" (meditations on a variety of subjects: "The Wonder of Change," "The Wonder of Attachments," etc.) will stir you in an indescribable manner. This is a bold and bright new kind of book that gently leads us on a journey of Spiritual Alchemy where the journey itself is the destination . . . and the destination is our need to be spiritually whole men and women.

Most of all, you will find out through self-investigation that we live in a friendly, intelligent and living universe that we can reach into and that can reach us.

0-87542-221-7
192 pp., 5¼ x 8, softcover $9.95